P9-DKE-650

Reading

with Babies,

Toddlers and

Twos

A Guide to Choosing, Reading and Loving Books Together

DISCARDED

CONCORD PUBLIC LIBRARY
45 GREEN STREET
CONCORD, NH 03301

Susan Straub, *Founder of* Read to Me
& KJ Dell'Antonia

SOURCEBOOKS, INC.®
NAPERVILLE, ILLINOIS

Copyright © 2006 by Susan Straub and KJ Dell'Antonia
Cover and internal design © 2006 by Sourcebooks, Inc.
Cover illustration© Judy Love
Internal permissions: Maral Rapp

Sourcebooks and the colophon are registered trademarks of Sourcebooks, Inc.

All rights reserved. No part of this book may be reproduced in any form or by any electronic or mechanical means including information storage and retrieval systems—except in the case of brief quotations embodied in critical articles or reviews—without permission in writing from its publisher, Sourcebooks, Inc.

This publication is designed to provide accurate and authoritative information in regard to the subject matter covered. It is sold with the understanding that the publisher is not engaged in rendering legal, account, or other professional service. If legal advice or other expert assistance is required, the services of a competent professional person should be sought.—From a Declaration of Principles Jointly Adopted by a Committee of the American Bar Association and a Committee of Publishers and Associations

All brand names and product names used in this book are trademarks, registered trademarks, or trade names of their respective holders. Sourcebooks, Inc., is not associated with any product or vendor in this book.

Published by Sourcebooks, Inc.
P.O. Box 4410, Naperville, Illinois 60567-4410
(630) 961-2168
Fax: (630) 961-2168
www.sourcebooks.com

Library of Congress Cataloging-in-Publication Data
Dell'Antonia, K. J.
  Reading with babies, toddlers, and twos : A guide to choosing, reading, and
loving books together / K. J. Dell'Antonia, Susan Straub.
     p. cm.
  Includes index.
  ISBN-13: 978-1-4022-0612-2
  ISBN-10: 1-4022-0612-7
  1. Reading (Preschool) 2. Infants--Books and reading. 3.
Toddlers--Books and reading. I. Straub, Susan. II. Title.

LB1140.5.R4D45 2006
372.4--dc22

2005033347

Printed and bound in the United States of America
CH 10 9 8 7 6 5 4 3 2

For my dear Peter, and for Ben & Emma
—*Susan*

To Rob, Sam, Lily, and Wyatt; and to Mom and
Dad (who read to me!)
—*KJ*

Acknowledgments

We are deeply grateful to our contributing families and to all the children's writers and illustrators who make our lives better with their artful work. Among the many kind and book-loving friends who gave us help, we'd like to especially thank:

Delia Battin
Pat Cummings
Michael Fusco
Kathy Kinsner
Deanna Pacelli
Rachel Payne
Holly L. L. Pierce

And finally, our heartfelt thanks to Joëlle Delbourgo, who believed in the idea of this book from the moment she saw it, and to Bethany Brown, Michelle Schoob, Dawn Pope, and the dedicated people at Sourcebooks who worked so hard to help us transform it into a reality.

Introduction:
Read Early, Read Often

Every book is its own world, and we'd like to welcome you to ours—a baby-centric, book-centered place. Here we sit, surrounded by piles of picture books, early storybooks, pop-up books, and the occasional book that moos if you accidentally step on it. We're always on the floor, reading and playing endless games of "what's that?" on every page. The more dog-eared the books are, the more we love them, and the more we love the babies, toddlers, and two-year-olds we read them with. So, welcome to our world in every sense—welcome to taping ripped pages and wiping off syrupy handprints and reading everything twenty times over. Welcome to a wonderful place where cats wear hats, ducks ride bicycles, and books mean as much to your baby as they do to you.

On average, children spend only forty-nine minutes with books per day compared with two hours and twenty-two minutes in front of a TV or computer screen. Want above-average kids? Read.

We all want to raise readers—kids with empathy for other characters (and people), kids with big vocabularies, kids with big imaginations, and kids who can always slide into another world with a book. But raising a child who reads doesn't start with teaching a child to read—in fact, it doesn't start with a child at all. It starts with a baby.

Do you remember being read to as a baby? Most memories of the reading experience, whether as a parent or a child, involve older children, preschoolers, and early readers. But the building blocks for that experience come from reading with babies, toddlers, and twos. From burpers and droolers, crawlers and cruisers, to walkers and talkers, these little people can love reading, too. But, like so many things, they can't do it without your help.

Ten Reasons to Read to Your Baby or Toddler

1. It's fun.
2. It builds vocabulary.
3. It stimulates the imagination.
4. It increases the chance of later academic success.
5. It teaches empathy and understanding of other viewpoints.
6. It entertains, it stimulates, and it lights up the senses (and it's not TV).
7. Books are portable and infinitely useful.
8. Reading is an introduction to our culture and our world.
9. It teaches, period.
10. It's fun!

A child who is read to from the very beginning is a child who will come into consciousness knowing that books are a source of pleasure and knowledge. She's a baby with a broad vocabulary and a broader experience—a city child who knows cows and a country kid who can hail a taxi. She's an art critic and a connoisseur of rhyme schemes. In short, she's a kid who's going places, because she's a baby who's been places, all in the comfort of your lap.

How to Use This Book

Every chapter of this book offers two things: a thorough look at a reading topic—from the basics of reading aloud to art appreciation in picture books—and book lists. A lot of book lists. We love these books. Susan's been choosing books for the READ TO ME Program (designed to encourage teen parents to read with their babies) for seventeen years, and she's learned through trial and error what grabs a baby's attention. Her observations have given her some insight into why babies like what they like. KJ's got a persnickety audience at home, and she's interviewed a whole host of other moms for their favorites and insights. We've also asked librarians, booksellers, and teachers for their lists of favorites. We asked them, "Why are some books carried around, colored on, taken to meals, and slept with, while others are pushed away after a single page?" We put all that together to create our lists—lists of New Classics, Activity Books, Pop-Ups, Bedtime Books, and Naming Books. We've also included anecdotes, general tips, and tips specific to reading with two kids in every chapter. The Ages and Stages charts show activities, techniques, and other scoop on reading with newborns, sitters, crawlers, cruisers, and walkers.

Sam's Top Ten

At the time of this writing, Sam is twenty-one months old and a voracious "reader." I've been reading to him since he was just a few days old. He's now beginning to appreciate longer narratives, but he clings to his old board book favorites as well. It takes a few readings for him to warm up to any book— he'll push it away, then go back to it after we've read a few familiar books instead. He especially likes books that feature some of his favorite things—moose, the moon, pancakes, and dogs. He will sit and read with me several times a day, often for thirty minutes or as long as I'm willing. He requests books by name and refers to them often throughout the day. I do find that he's more likely to like a book I like—probably because I persist with it.

—KJ

1. Anything with Max and Ruby

   (especially *Max's First Word* and *Max Cleans Up*)
2. *If You Give a Pig a Pancake*
3. *Harold and the Purple Crayon*
4. *The Great Gracie Chase*
5. *Clap Hands*
6. *Bedtime for Frances*
7. *Planes*
8. *Hondo and Fabian*
9. *The Big Book of Beautiful Babies Board Book*
10. *Chugga-Chugga Choo-Choo*

We asked some of the moms we met to tell us a little about their baby, and then give us a list of their baby's favorite books at that moment. Book clubs do this for older kids ("If you liked *Little House*, you might also like *Caddie Woodlawn*"), and websites do it for adults ("Customers who bought these selections also purchased..."). We're giving babies equal time. If you find a list that sounds like yours, or a baby that reminds you of your own, it might guide you to some new favorites.

Finally, we're both parents— Susan's raised two avid and successful readers. KJ's raising a preschooler who loves to read his books and a baby who still loves to eat them. We've learned from experience, and we've learned from experts (including plenty of expert parents we know and admire). In the end, all of the tricks, tips, hints, and true confessions you'll find here aim towards one thing: making reading with your baby or toddler fun for you both. We believe it's the best possible gift you can give your baby.

For Teachers and Caregivers

This book directly addresses the concerns and day-to-day lives of parents and other primary caregivers, but there's great information here for teachers and day-care providers as well. We hope you'll discover some new books for the shelves of your centers and classrooms and gain some insight into why certain books can be important or helpful to children at certain times. We also hope you'll use the book as a resource for helping the parents you work with. A parent who picks up this book is already planning to read to his or her child, but many parents aren't reading at home, or are limiting their reading to bedtime. You are in a perfect position to introduce those parents to the joys of reading with their child by letting them know how much their children enjoy certain books you've read in class, and by including book suggestions or reading tips in your newsletter or on your classroom news board. Other ideas include organizing a book drive for the classroom, suggesting parents buy two copies—one for class, one for home. You could also distribute information on local libraries with children's rooms and storytimes to parents and encourage them to meet at the library for a playdate. Parents turn to a trusted care provider for perspective and advice on their child's development as well as for care. We hope we can help you to introduce more parents to the joys of reading with their child.

Let's read!

—*Susan and KJ*

Chapter One:
Real Reading, Real Kids:
The Why, Who, and What

Before life presented you with an actual baby, you had a mental vision: A small, cuddly bundle in a blanket, sucking a finger and nodding off to sleep as she listens to you read. As you turn the last page, your voice softens, and you look down—she's out like a light. With a kiss on her soft cheek, you tuck her into her crib whispering, "Goodnight, Baby."

Sure, that happens—about once a year. Even a baby who loves to be read to isn't going to curl up in your lap every time. Sometimes other things and other needs will prevail, whether it's getting to the tempting toy across the room or demanding the breast or bottle—NOW! And sometimes it's urgent, for whatever reason, that you read the page with the picture of the pig with an umbrella first and only then start at the beginning of the book—or just go on from there. And sometimes the book has to be upside-down, or held just so, or held at an impossible angle by baby. Toddlers tear books. Twos throw them. Sometimes it seems like you spend more time baby-wrangling than reading. These are wonderful resources—but the truth is, it isn't the same. When you read together, you experience the world of the book together. You share points of reference, inside jokes, new cultures, new words, new experiences. You can't tune

Fun Things Babies Do While You Read

- Fall asleep
- Grab the book
- Pull your hair
- Hold the page so you can't turn it
- Sit on the floor and look at you like you're out of your mind
- Tear the page
- Throw the book on the floor
- Point and demand "what's that?" of every object on the page
- Scream
- Babble out her own story while you read
- Open and shut the book over and over for a little "peek-a-boo"
- Listen happily for two pages, then head off—and get upset if you stop reading!

out the world of the book you're reading to your child, and most of the time, you won't want to.

But while reading together may be fun, it won't always be perfect, and it will rarely happen exactly as you imagine it. You may think books are for reading. Your baby sees that books are almost infinitely useful for peek-a-boo, experimentation with Newton's Law of Gravity, and forming a bridge to allow the giraffe to walk into the plastic barn door. It seems as if there's an enormous gulf between what the two of you are trying to achieve. You're trying to get to the end of *Harold and the Purple Crayon*. Your baby is trying to taste the book cover. You want to read; she wants to experience. Her experience, though, is really akin to your reading. She's learning the book: as an individual book, a part of a larger set of books, as a hard object, a soft object, a paper object, and, finally, something that causes you to make a given set of sounds.

Whether she's tasting *Harold*'s cover or using him for a hat, she's happy. Isn't that what you really want—creativity, experimentation, imaginative play, talking and laughing and doing something together? Let go of the goal and savor the experience. You probably already know how it ends, anyway.

Why Read? Because You Like To, That's Why

If you didn't want to read to your baby, toddler, or two-year-old, it's not likely you'd have picked up this book. You've already decided you want to read together, but why? What will either of you take away from the time you spend together, book in hand? Reading is a pleasure you can share. It's one of the first activities you can enjoy together. You're not likely to be biking together for a while, after all. Reading can make raising your baby that much more wonderful. At its best, it's a chance to snuggle in tightly and quietly enter another world together. At the very least, it's a distraction from a difficult moment or a difficult day. Sometimes it's a last-ditch way to provide entertainment when you simply haven't got another creative thing left to give.

Researchers say that the number of different words a baby hears each day is the single most important predictor of later intelligence, school success, and social competence, if those words come from one of baby's special people—mother, daddy, grandma, nanny—rather than from a box on the wall. Reading counts.

To your child, though, reading is so much more than just fun. Life comes in via the senses. The world comes to your baby through her eyes, ears, nose, mouth, and fingers. Reading to your baby allows you to bring her even more aspects of that world in smaller, easily absorbed packages. A real truck is a big, scary, noisy thing to a four-month-old or even an eighteen-month-old. A truck on the pages of a book is small and predictable, something that can be held and controlled or sent away with a turn of the page. The same holds true for monsters and green peas. A book lets a baby take in the world on her own terms.

Books link kids to our world and our culture. *Winnie the Pooh, Curious George, Where the Wild Things Are, Chicken Soup,* Dr. Seuss—they're a backdrop for our world. A college professor complained recently that there's no shared frame of literary reference among her students—she can't assume that they all will have read *Great Expectations* or *To Kill a Mockingbird.* She can't have gone back far enough. Surely every student had read (or heard) some version of Cinderella! Familiar characters and their stories shape our view of places and things that, as a child, we haven't usually seen yet. Their experiences give us a framework for dealing with our own. As you read to your baby you welcome her into the culture that will become her own, and you can share other cultures with her as well.

{ *"I come home from work as a Head Start teacher exhausted and worried about putting dinner on the table and getting things done. My two-year-old is always tugging at my leg with a book. Finally, I just put everything down, sit on the floor, plop her into my lap, and read her book—and it's usually the best break of my day."* —Brenda }

Ten Picture Books We Dare You Not to Enjoy

1. **Cows Going Past**, Bruce Balan, Scott Nash (illus.). The view out the car window reveals clever cows doing some surprising things.

2. **What Can You Do with a Shoe?** Beatrice Schenk de Regniers, Maurice Sendak (illus.). Brother and sister duo find creative ways to play with a shoe, a chair, and a hat (and other things) in rhythmic verse.

3. **What James Likes Best,** Amy Schwartz. James is thrilled by the mundane on trips in and around the city.

4. **I Love Colors,** Margaret Miller. Big baby faces peek through and around colorful and familiar toys.

5. **The Hiccupotamus,** Aaron Zenz. There's fun in the colorful, antic illustrations and the travails of the hiccuping hippo as well as the nonsense rhymes.

6. **My Friends,** Taro Gomi. A little girl learns in very simple ways from animal and human friends.

7. **The Everything Book,** Denise Fleming. Something akin to a Richard Scarry book in the sheer amount of information and entertainment on every page, with gorgeously tactile illustrations.

8. **The Adventures of Taxi Dog,** Debra Barracca, Sal Barracca, Mark Buehner (illus.). Even kids who've never seen a taxi will enjoy the bright, graphic adventures of the dog who rides daily with his owner in a New York City cab.

9. **The Shirley Hughes Nursery Collection,** Shirley Hughes. We love her stories and artwork! These five concept books feature a wonderfully creative, curious child exploring her universe and tell simple stories in rhyme that toddlers really understand.

10. **No, David!,** David Shannon. Shannon's illustrations, roughly and childishly drawn, perfectly capture David's amazing knack for trouble as well as his charm. Popular with every kid who's ever heard that sudden shouted "No!"

Ned's Top Ten

"Ned, at two years, two months, is a big fan of books and totally wedded to our bedtime book routine. We usually read four to five books culminating with **How Do Dinosaurs Say Goodnight?** *(the current favorite for the past four months!). Recently, I have noticed that he is willing to sit for a bit longer in favor of some wordier books, but we still have our favorite board books that we have been reading since birth. Selfishly, I hope our nighttime ritual continues well into the future because I enjoy his reaction to the books sometimes more than I think he enjoys the stories! Lastly, I have noticed as we hit two that Ned was ready for books on tape. This has been a great way to take our favorites (see nine and ten on the list) with us while we are on the go!"*

—Kitty

1. How Do Dinosaurs Say Goodnight?
2. Joseph Had a Little Overcoat
3. Goodnight Moon
4. Planes, Trains, and Airport, all by Byron Barton
5. Moo, Baa, La La La! and others by Sandra Boynton
6. Train Song
7. Big Red Barn
8. Bark, George
9. Chicka Chicka Boom Boom
10. Fox in Sox

Will reading together teach your child to read faster? Will it put her ahead of the curve, get her into the right preschool, help her ace her SATs? There are no guarantees. We can tell you that nothing shows a baby or a child the importance of reading like a parent with a book in her hand. But we can also tell you that if reading becomes medicine (two books a day keeps the bad grades away), it ceases to be fun for either of you. Read together for pleasure, for the fun of shared rhymes, and the excitement of shared worlds. Anything else is just gravy.

Who Reads? Everybody.

The amazing thing about books—to a young child—is that every person says pretty much the same thing when they read the same book. In fact, that's one of the ways the baby knows a book IS a book. It may change a little (Mama laughs at the monkey, and the babysitter always says "zoom!"), but the art and the words and the feeling stay the same. She loves the continuity and the comfort of it. When her parents go out, Grandma or the babysitter can read a special book, and then Mama or Daddy can read it again when they get home. Toddlers can carry favorites with them as they go, and some two-year-olds even enjoy books on tape.

Encourage your babysitter or regular caregiver to read with your baby. Make it clear that books are part of the bedtime and naptime routine, and leave a stack of books in the room they generally play in or next to a bottle or snack.

What Should We Read? Great Literature and Cereal Boxes

What to read to kids under three is a subject that could fill a book (and it has—this one, among others listed in the appendix). But generally, the answer is *everything*. Maybe you're convinced that you only want to read quality stuff to your little one, and you've been avoiding Barney books like the plague. But here's the thing—to some extent, it's all good stuff. Many a reader of *Sweet Valley High* will grow up to read Jane Austen. Picture books work the same way. Most of the magic is in the act of reading itself, and a few, or even a few hundred, readings of something you consider to be poorly written, plotless, banal, or otherwise offensive to your sensibilities won't hurt anyone but you, and you're tough enough to take it.

> *"My mother has been reading* Hand, Hand, Fingers, Thumb *to two-year-old Brady since he was teeny tiny. Since she lives far away, she doesn't see him as often as we'd like. But I've been holding the phone up to his ear since he was just a few weeks old, and she always quotes it to him. We keep a copy at our house and one at her house, and when we visit her, or she visits us, it's one of the first ways they reconnect—by sitting down and reading 'Dum Ditty Dum Ditty Dum Dum Dum!'"*   —Amy

That said, not every book works for every child, or at every age. At least one librarian has told us she's constantly asked, "What should I read to my two-year-old? We're outgrowing board books, but most picture books are too long." Some books work better for certain ages. And some books are richer than others and just more fun to read. Because while your baby has tastes and quirks from day one, the books you choose can shape those tastes. And you'll be reading them almost as often as she will. You need books that work and books you'll both love. The rest of this book is devoted to helping you find them.

In the end, reading isn't just about books. Almost everything in our society is covered in words, from cereal boxes to

Featured Book

BOOK!

By Kristine O'Connell George,
Maggie Smith (illus.)

This is the book that proves our point. The baby in this book loves his book. He wears it and treats it like a favorite stuffed toy, taking it everywhere.

road signs. All make excellent reading in their own way, and begin to convey that reading is for fun *and* for information. Information is powerful stuff to a toddler. When you start thinking about reading throughout your day, don't forget that you already are—at the breakfast table, at the grocery store, in the car, and on a walk as you point out the signs and boxes that describe and direct us.

{ *"My eleven-month-old mostly likes to disrupt other people's reading: pulling newspapers off the table, taking a book out of your hand. His method is to either drop the reading material directly on the floor, or to turn it over in his hands a couple of times before dropping it on the floor. He also favors the inserts that the* New York Post *has been putting in the papers. They had recent series on the Yankees, the Jets, and animal wildlife. They're like magazines, glossy and full of big color photos, but only about six pages. I can tell from the way they are crumpled (and on the floor) that he has been the one enjoying them."* –Jennifer }

It never ceases to amaze us how much a good artist can convey with two dots and a line for a face. Helen Oxenbury is particularly gifted in this regard. Her round-headed babies, with their pants slipping off their chubby waists and their plump hands grasping spoons and drumsticks, look so simple you'll wonder why you can't draw something like that yourself—but you can't. We love her quartet of extra-large sized board books (*Clap Hands*; *Say Goodnight*; *Tickle, Tickle*; *All Fall Down*) featuring babies involved in their day-to-day activities—reading, eating, bathing, swinging—as well as the books aimed at the slightly older crowd, like *Tom and Pippo*. These books may make a great introduction to narrative for a baby who loves the early books, since his familiarity with Oxenbury's artwork will make the book that much more appealing and comforting.

The Classics
Twenty-five Picture Books for Every Child's Library

These are great books—books you'll find in every library, every preschool, every bookstore. You've probably heard of many of them; some you may remember from your own childhood and some you may read to your grandchildren someday.

1. ***Clifford the Big Red Dog,*** Norman Bridwell. Yes, it's a television series; yes, it's a franchise…but the original books are really good and perfect for babies and toddlers. Big, red dog. Need we say more?

2. ***Harold and the Purple Crayon,*** Crockett Johnson. You may remember Harold, but you probably didn't think of him as a book for very young babies. In fact, he works very well—simple illustrations and many moons.

3. **Goodnight Moon,** Margaret Wise Brown, Clement Hurd (illus.). The old-fashioned setting, the simple rhymes, and the cozy illustrations make this a nighttime must read for many toddlers.

4. **Big Red Barn,** Margaret Wise Brown, Felicia Bond (illus.). Evokes the author's *Goodnight Moon,* and offers a peaceful, lulling rhythm to a day on the farm. Simple drawings.

5. **Go, Dog. Go!,** P. D. Eastman. Simple books meant for beginning readers can make great books for beginning talkers.

6. **Pat the Bunny,** Dorothy Kunhardt. The mother of all interactive baby books.

7. **The Very Hungry Caterpillar,** Eric Carle. Kids love putting their fingers through the holes and pulling the pages to watch the hungry caterpillar eat his way through an uncomfortable assortment of food.

8. **Hop on Pop,** Dr. Seuss. A wonderful introduction to rhyme.

9. **Where's Spot?** Eric Hill. Plump, yellow Spot and his wonder at discovering the world around him have spoken to children for decades. Also available as *¿Dónde está Spot?* in Spanish, and in many other languages.

10. **Time for Bed,** Mem Fox, Jane Dyer, (illus.). Lovingly illustrated animal mothers cuddle their babies into sleep.

11. **The Little Fire Engine,** Lois Lenski. Fireman Small drives his old-fashioned fire engine to a comforting rescue.

12. **Guess How Much I Love You,** Sam McBratney, Anita Jeram (illus.). Big Nutbrown Hare can one-up Baby Nutbrown Hare's declarations of love every time, but this baby doesn't give up.

13. **Where the Wild Things Are,** Maurice Sendak. Sent to his room for being a wild thing, Max travels to the forest and conquers even wilder things before realizing that home is best.

14. ***Corduroy,*** Don Freeman. A lovely story of a little girl's kindness and empathy for a teddy bear who needs a home, with realistic illustrations.

15. ***Caps for Sale: A Tale of a Peddler, Some Monkeys, and Their Monkey Business,*** Esphyr Slobodkina. A wonderful, timeless tale of copying and cleverness.

16. ***Babies,*** Gyo Fujikawa. An appreciation of babies for and by babies and young children, without any adults pictured, with the kind of straightforward illustrations many kids love.

17. ***Harry the Dirty Dog,*** Gene Zion, Margaret Bloy Graham (illus.). Harry needs a bath—and after he's run away from one, he gets so dirty his family doesn't recognize him. His ultimate return and his family's recognition make for a very satisfying resolution.

18. ***Tikki Tikki Tembo,*** Arlene Mosel, Blair Lent (illus.). Why do Chinese children have short names, and not long, honorable ones? In this famous retold fairy tale, you'll discover a true marriage between story and art. And be prepared to have *tikki tikki tembo-no sa rembo-chari bari ruchi-pip peri pembo* become a refrain in your house.

19. ***George and Martha,*** James Marshall. The hippos have an admirable friendship, so real that it's full of pranks, hurt feelings, and make-ups. Marshall produced tons more brief stories about them, but this is the first. Arguably the story *Split Pea Soup* is a legend all by itself. Fun for the whole family.

20. ***The Little House,*** Virginia Lee Burton. Most of us remember the poignant illustrations in this story of a little house in the country that becomes surrounded by city before sympathetic owners move it to the country again.

21. ***Mike Mulligan and His Steam Shovel,*** Virginia Lee Burton. No toddler can resist the story of Mike and his steam shovel Mary Anne digging all through the day to prove they're just as good as the more modern machines.

22. ***Blueberries for Sal,*** Robert McCloskey. This simply illustrated glimpse of the past resonates with any child who's lost sight of Mom as Sal does during blueberry picking. Most modern kids have followed the wrong set of legs at least once and will enjoy the story of how Sal manages to follow a bear.

23. ***The Little Engine That Could,*** Watty Piper. This tale still resonates, and always will. The original illustrations are fun, and if the words (definitely a little on the sweet and cloying side) begin to get to you, you can always edit a bit.

24. ***Curious George,*** H. A. Rey. The story of the little monkey, so like a toddler in his curiosity and impulsiveness but so much more capable, is one kids love. You'll probably notice now that George's removal from the jungle isn't the most politically correct thing ever written, but your child won't mind.

25. ***Whistle for Willie,*** Ezra Jack Keats. A whistle will call Willie the dog, but Peter can't whistle until practice finally pays off. Refreshingly warm collage illustrations.

Ages and Stages: Getting Started

This chart suggests tips on reading to babies as they develop. Up to a point, these stages are sequential. For example, your baby will sit before she crawls, and crawl or creep or scoot before she walks. Later development is less predictable. Many a baby is madly running off into the parking lot long before she's forming two word sentences, or piping up with "Why he crying, Mama?" but unable or unwilling to climb a ladder. Verbal and physical development can vary wildly during the toddler years, and we've tried to account for that by suggesting different tips or activities for the wild child and the precocious talker.

The point is to have fun with babies and books. Focus on what the baby CAN do for maximum success.

Newborn	• She is absorbing every word…and absorbing is a good way to put it, because for the most part, those words are just sounds to her—sounds that are developing her mind and sparking the synapses she needs to speak English or Chinese (or whatever language she's hearing). But at this age, she's every bit as happy to hear you read aloud from *Sports Illustrated,* although neither the content nor the illustrations will truly satisfy.
	• Try black and white books or books with just a few colors, and leave the page open for as long as she wants to look at the picture.
	• Find books with texture and help her to pat the bunny or feel the cat's sandy tongue.

Heads Up	• Try putting her on the floor with an open book in front of her for "tummy time." • Offer her one book to hold (or munch) while you read another.
Sitting	• A good time to start "Where is the____? There it is!" • Sit across from each other on the floor and hand books back and forth. Talk about them—"Can I have the book with the doggie? Thank you!"
Crawling/Creeping	• Relax—action may win over reading for the next few months. If you find yourselves struggling, save books for quiet moments, like pre-nap and bed. She WILL tire, and she WILL need a break (and so will you). • Let the baby crawl to you and a book as you read. • Try reading a book with baby in the high chair after a meal.
Cruising/Walking	• This is a prime time for insisting on one "favorite" book. Exact repetition is deeply comforting at this stage! • This is a big time for throwing books, too. Books are toys but not balls! It's probably time to stop reading and try another game.

Talking (a few words)	• Baby may have one favorite word for everything in the book and everywhere else, like *boggie*. Be patient and try distinguishing cat-*boogie*, dog-*boggie*, and gramma-*boggie*.
	• Try books with animals to let both of you practice making animal sounds.
	• Baby may want to read to you! Enjoy the reading even though upside down, backwards, and unintelligible. Listen, smile, laugh.
	• Look for books that feature a favorite word, like ball or dog or moon. You may be able to bring out something a little longer and more complicated just because it has a moose on every page.
Talking More	• Now you can play "Where is the____?" and wait for your answer! Be patient—try not to help until she's really stumped. Ask about the less obvious things on the page, too.
	• BABY POWER! WANT BOOK NOW! Well, why not take a little reading break? If you agree right away, it's not giving in to whining, it's just saying yes to a particularly insistent question.
Running (but not talking much)	• These balls of energy can be as hard on books as they are on shoes. Get out the tape and try not to let it bother you too much. If you get really upset over an accidental page tear or the beheading of the pop-up pig, reading may become a game your child won't want to play any more.
	• Remember that thought processes probably exceed vocabulary if your child is in this stage. Try to choose some more complex books for quiet times, maybe with a focus on something your

baby loves to hear about, like farms or trucks.

- Incorporate some physical activity into a reading session. "Can you run and bring me a ball like the one on the page? That bunny is jumping—can you show me how you jump?"

- Serious wigglers may try to interact with the book with their feet, too. We don't know why—something about having the book right where she can reach up and kick it (like when she's reading on your lap or you're lying down together) is too much temptation. If you can, just move the book out of range and ignore it. Try not to turn it into a battle of wills that takes attention away from the book!

Talking ALL THE TIME!

- Expand those questions. "Can you find something red? Can you find something the bear could eat? What do you think the mouse will do with the crayons?"

- Try to get your toddler to tell you the stories from her favorite books.

- Try getting something wrong in a book and letting her catch you. Start with something egregious—No! That's not an elephant!

- Don't put aside the baby books just because your baby is talking like an older child. Leave them where she can choose to keep patting the bunny if she wants.

- Try some classic Winnie the Pooh—longer stories, smaller illustrations that don't tell the story. But don't worry if at first it doesn't take.

Chapter Two:
Now: A Very Fine Time to Start

After "What do I read?" the number two question about reading to a baby is "When should we start?" The answer is simple: Now. Whether you've got a new walker, a gazing infant, or even a baby in utero, now is the time to pick up a book and start reading. Reading aloud works at every age and stage.

Reading to the Bump in the Belly

You may laugh, but your baby's listening. Researchers from the University of North Carolina set out to prove it by asking mothers to read a selected passage from Dr. Seuss's *The Cat in the Hat* daily to their babies in utero at between thirty-two and thirty-seven weeks gestation. At thirty-eight weeks in the womb and in the days immediately after their birth, they tested the babies for recognition of the passage and found that babies preferred the familiar passages to unfamiliar ones read by the same voice. (Unborn babies showed their preference with a more relaxed heart rate, newborns by modifying their sucking patterns to keep listening to the familiar part of the story.) Other studies have shown a preference in the womb for the native language and for familiar voices and songs. Our conclusion? Read to her, sing to her, talk to her. Choose a book or a song and repeat it over and over, and you'll have a head start on soothing your baby when she enters the world.

> *"I just knew they could hear music," says Mark, now the father of two girls, ten and eight. "I used to put a speaker on my wife's belly so the baby could listen with us. I tried to pick music that would sound good under water, since that's how I imagined the baby would hear it. We had a lot of fun, listening to new things, talking to the baby."*

Did we read to our bellies? Well, no. Susan remembers talking aloud to her babies before they were born. She told them what she was doing and asked questions about who they were and what they were doing in there. Mostly she was just carrying on a one-sided conversation, much as she did when Emma and Ben were infants (and again when they were teenagers, but that's another story). KJ did the same. While we may not have actually read to our babies in utero, we were sharing our day and our stories and recognizing our babies, even before they left our bodies, as their own individual selves. Reading to a baby in utero is just one of the many ways a mother-to-be can communicate.

Dads are different. They may not be able to chat with the unborn baby throughout the day, but many are still eager to get into the act. Dad may love

FEATURED BOOK

Oh, Baby, the Places You'll Go!
A Book to be Read in Utero

Tish Rabe

This clever short book adapts pieces of nearly all of Dr. Seuss for reading to babies still in the womb.

reading to the "bump." By reading to the baby, he's nourishing and nurturing him in a different way. Many dads relish their role as teacher and as the great introducer of new and cool things, and what could be cooler than Dr. Seuss? Your baby will recognize Dad's voice from straight out of the womb, just as he'll recognize many of the sounds that have become familiar over the past nine months. If Dad's been reading or singing to him, he may find the music of his voice even more comforting in a strange new world.

Newborns: The Perfect Audience

For those few months after birth, your baby is absorbing everything around her. As you read to her, she's taking in all of the sounds and rhythms that make up her native language. Caught in the right mood, she'll gaze at you in worship no matter what you read.

"Reading (unlike most things) has made me feel powerful as a parent— especially during those first few weeks when every experience feels brand new. As a first-time mom, there are so many situations I had simply never been forced to deal with before Olivia's arrival. Though my husband and I were well-acquainted with parenting theories and had read about infant development, I was amazed by how much is simply 'on the job' training. Reading is something I know how to do. I may need to alter my style or improvise the story to keep her interest, but I do know how to read. It is frankly just so nice to have an outlet where you can feel confident as a parent, even when there seem to be so many uncertainties." —Michelle

Newborns may make an easy audience, but parents usually have a lot of questions about reading to them. They may not be difficult to read to, but they're not terribly responsive, either. Here are a few of the questions we hear most often.

My newborn baby seems calm and content and happy with the reading one minute, but in the blink of an eye starts horribly wriggling, writhing, and making fussy noises. I can't figure her out. What can I do?

This is classic! There is no clear answer as to what's going on with your baby. Is it hunger, digestion, discomfort, need to shift position, early memories of her birth, annoyance, even wordless rage? Try again another time.

Try reading to your older child when you nurse or feed your baby, so that she doesn't feel left out of the magic circle. Instead, it can be a special nurturing time for her, too.

Does it matter what I read to a very tiny infant?

Nope! Do you remember the Tom Selleck character in *Three Men and a Baby*, reading an account of a boxing match to the tiny baby girl on his lap? It's the wonderful sound of your voice that matters at that age, not the actual content.

What's she getting out of this, anyway?

She's getting an introduction to books and language. She's getting your undivided attention without having to cry for it, or even perform for it. She's getting a safe snuggle in your arms that's not related to feeding, or burping, or rocking, but just to being together while the words wash over and around her. If she likes it, consider it an early investment in a fabulously calming activity you can share for a long time to come.

If you want reading, storytelling, and the amazing world of the imagination to be a part of your child's very being, if you want books to be part of the air she breathes, read early, and read often. You'll have a baby who's never known—and can't imagine—a world without books.

TALKING WITH THE AUTHOR VERA B. WILLIAMS

I remember trying to share a book with my first baby and feeling foolish. But there would be one tiny minute when her attention was caught by the rhythm of some words or by a bit of red or person-like shape on the page. I'd see delight fleet across her ever-changing little face, and was hooked into sharing books with this tiny dawning literacy. Of course the very next minute she'd wrench the book from my hands to suck on the binding. But little by little, we two became a reading pair. I loved that. She would come toddling over dragging a book, plop it down into my lap, put her cheek by mine, and say, "READ ME." The combination is irresistible. The affection in the voice. The sing-song of it. The safe sense of an encircling arm (my mother's was covered with fascinating freckles), the snuggle of it, the adventure of turning the pages. My mother worked long hours. . . worried about money. She had limited time for me but every now and then I would crawl onto her lap and we would be together with *Here's a Ball for Baby* or *Cantaloupe for Breakfast,* chanting "Honey and a bun…" I'm seventy-eight years old and I still own the rhythms and images of those little verses from my first times with books and my mother.

The Sure-Fire Baby-Shower Booklist

Even if it doesn't matter what you read to a newborn, it's great to have some good baby books around. These books are the ultimate for baby gift giving, all guaranteed to please new moms and babies. You can be sure of heartfelt thanks before the first year is over.

- ***"More More More," Said the Baby,*** Vera B. Williams
- ***The Big Book of Beautiful Babies***, David Ellwand
- ***Hug,*** Jez Alborough
- ***Clap Hands, Say Goodnight, All Fall Down*** and ***Tickle, Tickle,*** Helen Oxenbury
- ***Sam's Book of Words,*** Yves Got
- ***Everywhere Babies,*** Susan Meyers, Marla Frazee (illus.)

Book in Hand, Book in Mouth: Reading with (Slightly) Older Babies

Grasping something in his hand is a big milestone for baby. Once it's in his hand, it seems to go straight into his mouth, quick. This makes reading hard. Feeding, changing, buckling the car seat all become more of a challenge. He's helping; he's hindering; he's making you crazy.

Try a cloth book to distract and entertain baby on the changing mat (and keep her hands out of the mess!).

It's wonderful to see your baby developing a personality and beginning to engage you. It's also a challenge. Now he can poke a finger into your eye and pinch your skin. Every day it becomes clearer that this isn't just a doll to dress and soothe. It's a real live little person with a very different idea of what to do with that sock. So, get that baby something else to do with those hands. He'll need something to explore with his fingers and mouth while you're reading, too. A pacifier, if you use one, a teething biscuit if he's ready for them, or any of his small toys could work. Another book might be even better. When he takes yours, you could switch to reading his.

{ *Kendall, mother of Eli, six months, describes the reading scene in Eli's world: "I gave Eli a book the other day in his high chair, and he was sitting there, turning the big pages, and I thought, Oh, he's so advanced! Just then, he grabbed the book in both hands, holding it open, and brought it up—SMACK—into his forehead as hard as he could."* }

Books with pictures of other babies (photos or simple drawings) usually intrigue babies at this age, as do big, colorful pictures. Of course, if it interests him, he'll just be more anxious to put the book in his mouth. Fabric books with crinkly pages and other textures can be touched, squeezed, chewed, and read, and he can usually hold them more easily than the board kind. Read from longer books while he's playing on the floor and recite nursery rhymes while you bounce him on your knee. You're learning to read to him, and he's learning to be read to. There's no rush. You've got plenty of time to get to *Huckleberry Finn*.

Starting with Photo Books

Mama's face is arguably the first (and the most beautiful) image a baby sees. Photographs of faces are a natural next step. You can show photos to your baby and talk about them. All you need to do is start. If you really think about it, isn't a collection of photographs in an album a book?

Some of the best books for babies and toddlers are indeed photo books of faces and daily life. Books of photographs appeal to all ages. Freed from printed words, pictures open up our imaginations. We get a breath of the person or place. Babies like to see other babies, and can spot a look-alike or a friend early on. When babies see these portraits, they mimic the smile or knit their brows in empathy with a miserable little face. They talk to these other babies the best way they can. Babies become very experienced very soon at reading faces. They pick up a whole universe of information very fast.

Some other books that include fun faces and babies:

- **Mrs. Mustard's Baby Faces,** Jane Wattenburg.
  This accordion fold out is an entertaining gem: happy floating baby heads on one side, and crabby cranky crying babies on the flip.
- **Peekaboo Baby,** Margaret Miller.
  Baby-face-sized photographs of baby faces with colorful props.
- **Baby! Talk!,** Penny Gentieu.
  Each page shows a set of babies acting out a favorite starter word or phrase, from "Go" to "Uh-Oh" to "So Big!"
- **Smile! (¡Sonríe!),** Roberta Grobel Intrater.
  Page-sized baby faces flirt with the camera. (And also other Baby Faces Board Books *Peek-a-boo!, Eat!, Splash!,* and in Spanish, *¡Cucú!, ¡Que Rico!,* and *¡Al Agua Patos!*)
- **Happy Baby: 123,** Roger Priddy.
  Big bright photos of favorite baby things.
- **Daddy and Me,** Neil Ricklen.
  All kinds of daddies loving all kinds of babies.

But She's Not Listening!
Reading to Sitters and Crawlers

At every stage, it's important to put aside your preconceived notions of what reading to your child will be like. What you may perceive as "problems" with the reading experience are actually stages of development. Sitting babies are going to grab the book, fall on the book, roll on the book, and drop the book. Crawlers are going to crawl away, crawl back, crawl away, crawl back. From the baby's perspective, this couldn't be better! She can keep your attention and listen to a story while she's on the move. But as the reader, you may feel frustrated with what seems to be an ungrateful audience. Your first instinct may be to put the book away and wait for a better time. Don't. People of all ages like to keep busy while they listen. Older kids may color during read-aloud time. Students doodle during lectures. You might knit while watching TV. If you think she's still tuned in, keep going. If she's clearly engrossed in taking apart the remote control, maybe it's time to stop.

Supporting herself and beginning to move are incredibly big moments for your baby. If she can sit up, she can really use her hands to explore what's in front of her. If a dropped toy skitters away, it's a huge thrill to finally be able to go after it. Make books part of the fun. Spread out a few for her to crawl or roll to while you sit and read from one. Choose books that focus on single objects so that you can show her ball and dog. Try sitting across from each other and handing books back and forth, or just handing them to baby. For real reading, bedtime and naptime may provide you with a quiet audience, and mealtime, if your baby can feed herself at all, may also work well.

> *"Last night, I was reading eleven-month-old Cole* But Not the Hippopotamus—*repeatedly. He was enjoying it, but I was getting tired of it. So I started reciting another one of his books,* Snuggle Puppy *(still turning the pages of* Hippopotamus*). Darned if he didn't immediately crawl over to the appropriate book and hold it up for me. Clever boy!"*
> —Doug

At this stage, babies are beginning to understand more about the world around them and to make some simple predictions. When the babysitter shows up, Daddy will leave. When the blanket sleeper goes on, bed is coming. You may find she's beginning to recognize both the reading ritual and certain books, as well.

Language is also beginning to seep in. Parents who've been using sign language may begin to see those signs from the baby, as well as other indications that she understands what you say. Books that identify objects will take on a renewed importance for her as her understanding increases. You will find, to your joy, that you are beginning to communicate with your baby with words.

Try taking a verbal break and just turn the pages for your baby while she looks at the pictures. Give her time to find her own story in the artwork.

Day-in-a-life books by writer-illustrators like Helen Oxenbury, Rachel Isadora, and Martha Alexander are wonderful for this stage and the next few to come. They create a kind of memory book for a small child. They may not seem very dramatic, and there's often no story. Instead they offer a series of snapshots from a baby's day. Every day is a long day to a baby, full of good times (eating, drinking, nursing, observing, playing) and frustrations (can't pull up, can't reach the toy, can't tell anyone why you're unhappy). These simple little books allow babies to think about their own experiences, which are often strange and new for the baby, no matter how ordinary they seem to us. These are likely to be the REAL baby books—the ones you probably won't be reading two years from now.

Simple Books about Baby's Day

- **Bedtime,** Kate Duke. The guinea pig heroes become less and less resistant to bedtime as it grows later.

- **Sam Loves Kisses,** Yves Got. Blocky and brightly colored Sam the bunny gets kisses from all the people he loves, leading up to a snuggly kiss at bedtime.

- **Pants Off First!,** Ruth Ohi. A toddler gets himself ready for bed while his clever pets distract him.

- **Lulu's Busy Day,** Caroline Uff. This little girl has a very active day with friends, artwork, housework, dinner, and a bath.

- **Bye Bye, Daddy,** Harriet Ziefert and Lisa Campbell Ernst. Baby Bunny rolls to the bakery and back again in the stroller, with familiar sights along the way.

- **My Mommy and I,** PK Hallinan. If a day with Mommy is a fun-filled romp, then this depicts a typical day. Even if it's a bit rosy, it's still a pleasure to a child to be so closely linked with Mom.

- **Blankie,** Leslie Patricelli. Blankie accompanies baby through food, nap, and play.

- **Busy Baby,** Fiona Watt, Catherine-Anne Mackinnon (illus.). Bright pastel images of a busy baby's day, with a touch of interactivity.

- ***The Baby's Catalogue: Baby Sleeps,*** Allen Ahlberg, Janet Ahlberg (illus.). Simple line illustrations take us through baby's day.

- ***Me Baby, You Baby,*** Ashley Wolff. Same rhymes and activities and love for two different families (one black, one white) through a day with their beloved babies.

- ***Peekaboo Morning,*** Rachel Isadora. A baby plays a game of peekaboo with his whole household, with the baby peeking out of an activity on one page and a lovely drawing in rich pastels of what he's peeking at on the next.

- ***Good Morning, Baby,*** Cheryl Willis Hudson, George Ford (illus.). A toddler and her daddy enjoy a day together. (Also *Good Night, Baby.*)

The Upright Baby Brigade: Movers and Shakers

Babies who can pull up and walk are babies with a lot going on and very little ability to talk about it. So much is happening to them physically that they may regress in other areas. They might start waking more often at night, and be unable to sit still or calm themselves. This goes for new crawlers as well. Both may become newly frustrated with their inability to communicate their needs or achieve their objectives. A familiar book and a comfortable lap might help to distract him from all those new bodily sensations when he's exhausted, or it might just seem like restraint. If he can't hold still in your lap, he can listen as he moves around the room. Perhaps you can shift to rhyming and song books, and make reading a lively, physical activity.

> *"Henry and Gus (two-year-old twins) add high drama to any reading experience. They play tug-of-war with their board books and rip the flaps off* Where is Maisy? *At this point all the favorite books are taped together, and several have had to be bought anew. I'm on my third copy of* Goodnight Moon. *I loathe that little book, but Henry picks it out of the pile and drags it around with him, going, 'Good-good-good-good-good.'"*
> —Judith

Some days, giving a child with little language and no self-control so much mobility can seem like a huge design flaw. It may take all of your energy to protect and divert him. There will be times when your new mover just can't get up and go (at the doctor's office, on an airplane, at a restaurant). A book is the perfect portable toy—it can be read in multiple ways and it can be the center of a variety of games (some of which have nothing to do with its literary qualities). It's good to play with together or it can be company for the baby alone in his stroller or car seat. A book with flaps can provide a fidgety child with a physical activity that doesn't take up much room. Board books are small, durable, and relatively light; paperback books even lighter, and just one can get you through the most boring (for baby) situation.

This is a good time to take a look at where your books are. If there are books in every room your baby spends time in, you'll read to your baby more often. You can turn to a book when other activities have run out of steam, and she can ask for a book with gestures or words when she needs a little quiet or a little cuddle. She'll learn that books aren't just meant to put you to sleep. They're a part of everyday life and can be just as—if not more—fun as any electronic button pushing gizmo the toy companies can devise. Best of all, a book is a surefire way to get grown-up participation and attention. Who can resist a request to read?

Olivia's Top Ten

Reading to Olivia (three months) has been a wonderful learning experience for both of us and is an activity we have shared since she was born. What began as a quiet and relatively passive activity on her part, undertaken mostly when she was sleepy or to calm her when fussy, has now become an incredible bonding experience. Over the months, I've watched Olivia's interest in reading pick up tremendously; she has gone from simply watching my facial expressions to making many of her own. Liv is now such an active participant in our reading sessions, often "helping me" to turn the pages and always reacting to something (usually with a high-pitched shriek of delight), whether it is simply the color on the page or the inflection in my voice. As we read some of her favorites together, I could swear that I sense her anticipation as we near her favorite parts of the story! Through all of this, I feel as though I have really been able to learn about my baby in a unique way and understand just what excites her. That is priceless.

1. **The Very Hungry Caterpillar**, Eric Carle. Her favorite.

2. **Mister Seahorse**, Eric Carle. About a daddy taking care of his seahorse babies—it is way over her head but amazingly illustrated and a sweet way to introduce real science.

3. **Motown Baby Love Board Books: #6: The Way You Do the Things You Do**, Charles R. Smith Jr. (photographer).

4. **Motown Baby Love Board Books: #8: Pride and Joy**, Charles R. Smith Jr. (photographer). Liv loves to have me sing these books to her, plus the parents are of many different ethnicities. She often squeals when she looks at the different pictures—so much fun! I'm likely to run out and buy them all pretty soon!

5. **Horton Hatches the Egg**, Dr. Seuss. She LOVES this book and even though it is long, sits through the whole thing rather patiently. I think it has something to do with the black-white-red illustrations and rhythmic nature of the verse.

6. **You and Me, Little Bear; Can't You Sleep, Little Bear? and Let's Go Home, Little Bear**, Martin Waddell, Barbara Firth (illus.). We all love these books—they are just sweet and show real parent-child situations (not that Liv knows that yet). She just likes the bear illustrations and soothing repetition in the stories. I think we'll be reading these for a long time to come.

7. **Good Night, Gorilla**, Peggy Rathmann. Liv seems to be particularly interested in animals right now and is a BIG fan of the gorilla. We have given this book to many friends over the years and all report that it has quickly become a favorite, right through the toddler years.

8. **I Love You, Little One**, Nancy Tafuri. Wonderfully rhythmic verse and sweet responses from the animal mommies.

9. **What Color Is Love?**, Linda Strachan. A sweet introduction both to colors and the more advanced concept of love truly being color-blind.

10. **Good Night, Little Bear**, Richard Scarry (illus.). A nice bedtime story featuring a daddy.

Happy Birthday!

The huge birthday party, with games and favors and a pile of presents, is likely to be overwhelming for a two- or three-year-old. Why not hold a "book swap party" instead? Ask each guest (well, the parent of each guest) to bring a gift-wrapped favorite book. Compare notes first, to make sure no one's going to get a duplicate, then give each child a book to unwrap. A willing adult can read the books to an enthralled circle, and each child goes home with a gift book.

Add to a library at your day care or preschool. Each birthday child could donate a book on her birthday, and be the first allowed to borrow it.

Many toddlers will enjoy choosing a favorite book to share, and it's fun to see what other families are reading. You may discover a new favorite. Meanwhile, an approaching birthday calls for topical reading. Try these:

- *Max's Birthday,* Rosemary Wells. A very simple story that manages, in just a few lines, to remind kids that what's scary at first can also be thrilling, and then delightful.

- *Happy Birthday, Moon,* Frank Asch. A story more about giving a gift than getting one.

- *Birthday Swap,* Loretta Lopez. A sympathetic sister offers a wonderful present: to trade her own summer date this year with her sibling's winter-time birthday.

- *Oscar's Half Birthday,* Bob Graham. Having achieved a six months milestone, Oscar's family cannot wait any longer to celebrate. It's a wonderful party.

- *Mr. Rabbit and the Lovely Present,* Charlotte Zolotow, Maurice Sendak (illus.). A little girl asks for Mr. Rabbit's advice about a present for her mother. As they talk and walk, a basket of lovely and colorful fruits becomes the satisfying answer. Thinking works.

- *It's My Birthday,* Helen Oxenbury. A little girl gathers ingredients from her animal friends, and shares both the cooking and the party with them. A gentle, repeating rhythm book about the making of a cake.

- *If You Give a Pig a Party,* Laura Numeroff, Felicia Bond (illus.). Whether it's a birthday party or any other celebration, nothing will go quite as expected when Numeroff and Bond's Pig (and her friends Moose and Mouse) are around, except that it will all come full circle in the end. Vividly detailed illustrations and the slightly complicated cause and effect story make this good for two-year-olds and up.

From Those First Few Words to Compound Sentences

Talking is where babies veer off from a consistent development curve. They have to roll before they can crawl and pull up before they can walk, but those first few words could come in almost anywhere. You'll already be seeing signs that she knows what you are saying to her. She may be able to hand you the red book or the dog book or pick out the appropriate book from the box. Her vocabulary is growing exponentially, and her understanding increases every day.

> *"I remember watching a friend get both her kids ready to go out. While her mom was push-guiding the active ten-month-old's arm into the sleeve of his jacket, and trying to prevent him from escaping from his stroller, Ellie, two and a half, noticed her shoelace was untied. 'Oh, Lewis,' she said aloud. Her mother kept working on the baby's wraps but commented, 'Oh dear. What's happened?' This was a remarkable communication! Ellie was referring to a favorite book—* Oh, Lewis! *by Eve Rice. In the book, everything goes wrong for Lewis, from his mittens to his jacket zipper to his whole day. The refrain 'Oh, Lewis!' is uttered by the exasperated, but understanding, mother at each difficulty. Ellie was describing a potential frustration, using a literary reference—and trying hard not to demand too much attention at an inconvenient moment. As it happened, I could offer to help, since I too knew the reference."* —Susan

Now is a wonderful time to zero in on those first words and start reading slightly longer books that feature those items prominently. Books that identify objects are wonderful, but more complex books—books that are introducing concepts like tomorrow and waiting and home—do just as much if not more to help her to understand the things she sees and hears. You may not see the benefit in her speech for months (or even years), but reading together exposes her not just to new words that might not come up in her daily life but also to concepts and speaking styles. She's absorbing it all.

Books for Babies with a Word or Two (Ball! Dog! Cat!)

- **Sam's Ball,** Barbro Lindgren, Eva Eriksson (illus.). Sam is wonderfully insistent, especially when his ball is eyed by the cat.

- **The Story of Red Rubber Ball,** Constance Kling Levy, Hiroe Nakata (illus.). This abandoned ball is investigated by any number of richly painted animals until a dog takes it home for keeps.

- **Lisa's Airplane Trip,** Anne Gutman, Georg Hallensleben (illus.). A dog (Dog!) takes a first trip on a plane (Plane!).

- **Happy Baby: Words,** Roger Priddy. Each page showcases one item with a beautiful picture and adds a sentence and a question about it.

- **Bright Baby's First 100 Words,** Roger Priddy. Cut out photographs set against bright paper highlight first words.

- **Touch and Feel: Kitten,** DK Pub. Come and feel the kitten's soft fur.

- **Clifford's Kitten,** Norman Bridwell. The big red dog takes care of a kitten.

Book games will expand her vocabulary even further and give her a chance to surprise you with her prowess. You may not even realize she knows the word "bee" until she's pointing at one in a book. Even while you're bringing in more complex books, keep reading the simple ones. A short book with just a few pictures and identifying words will probably be the first book she can "read" to you.

Books also give you and your new talker a shared frame of reference. Getting dressed books can become favorite jokes as you dress your child. Quoting from a favorite book as you perform a similar activity helps a child remember the book and draw comparisons between her life and the life the book shows.

IRRESISTIBLE AUTHORS — YVES GOT

Yves Got's books about Sam the bunny (*Sam Loves Kisses*, *Sweet Dreams, Sam*, etc.) are sweet without being cloying and the illustrations are very simply drawn, with thick black outlines and bright primary colors. Most fall into the daily activity book category, yet the pictures themselves offer rich fodder for narrative—why are Grandma and Grandpa giving tickle kisses? Is that present for Sam? What's his teddy bear doing? Got has also illustrated two delightful word books, *Sam's First Word Book* and *Sam's Big Book of Words*. At least one reviewer complains that *Sam's First Word Book* is much too long and uses terms that are too sophisticated for its audience—but actually, that's exactly what's great about it. With one hundred plus words, you can read it and riff on it for a very long time before your baby gets bored, making it a perfect travel companion. Babies and toddlers today probably know "remote control" and "computer" as well as "spoon" and "bowl" and welcome new words and images like "lipstick" and "convertible." *Sam's Big Book of Words* is a more advanced word book, with multiple words and images on each page. Got's books truly work for babies, toddlers, and twos.

The New Classics
(And Some Old Ones You May Have Forgotten)

You won't find *Goodnight Moon, Guess How Much I Love You,* or *Pat the Bunny* on our list of the new classics. Why not? Because those are the books you already own; the ones you had to return because your baby got three copies as gifts. These are the new classics—books that may not be on your shelves yet but that we think have real staying power, or older books that are still around but aren't necessarily on everyone's list. These are the books and authors that kept appearing over and over again on our moms' lists and were brought up repeatedly by booksellers and librarians.

- ***The Big Book of Beautiful Babies,*** David Ellwand. This is the best of many wonderful photo books of baby faces. We love the rhyme, the fact that it's black and white, and that it shows crying faces as well as happy faces.

- ***"More More More," Said the Baby,*** Vera B. Williams. Three beautiful, multicultural love stories between babies and their caregivers. If you could only have one book, this would have to be one you'd consider. (We should note that the board book can be hard to read, because the small text in many-colored letters just doesn't stand out as well as it does in the larger versions.)

- ***Baby Says,*** John Steptoe. Susan's favorite sibling story—a baby in a crib communicates with his brother via teddy bear. Simple realistic illustrations.

- ***Bear Snores On,*** Karma Wilson, Jane Chapman (illus.). Beautiful first story book with a great winter theme. Nice for a first step beyond board books. Big, colorful illustrations.

- ***Hondo and Fabian,*** Peter McCarty. A dog, a cat, and a baby have a very ordinary day, beautifully but simply illustrated (Caldecott nominee). Baby will like the soothing, repetitive words and pictures, and adults will like the subtle humor. Small, with (relatively) sturdy pages.

- **If You Give a Moose a Muffin,** Laura Numeroff, Felicia Bond (illus.). Silly and somehow universally appealing, even though it's fairly complex. Lots of babies really like moose! (Also *If You Give a Pig a Pancake*, *If You Give a Pig a Party* and *If You Give a Mouse a Cookie*.)

- **Owl Babies,** Martin Waddell, Patrick Benson (illus.). Perfect starter book for separation issues.

- **Chicka Chicka Boom Boom,** John Archambault and Bill Martin, Lois Ehlert (illus.). Fills the alphabet with personality. The rhyme and rhythm are unbeatable, and we wouldn't be surprised if young fans begin pointing out individual letters at a very early age. (*Note that the board book, which is available, omits half of the book. We suggest getting the larger version and saving it until your baby is ready to move past the board book stage.)

- **Chugga-Chugga Choo-Choo,** Kevin Lewis, Daniel Kirk (illus.). Introduces a fun concept—that the words on the page aren't necessarily exactly consistent with the pictures. The words describe a real train, but the pictures show a toy train traveling around a little boy's bedroom. The fact that the little boy shown only at the end is dark-skinned is a bonus—it's always good to see books that can reflect a multi-cultural society without being ABOUT a multi-cultural society.

- **How Do Dinosaurs Say Goodnight?,** Jane Yolen, Mark Teague (illus.). This is one of those big, fabulously illustrated books librarians read aloud at storytimes, but it also makes a great bedtime read. Worth springing for because this book will work really well with older kids, too—each dinosaur is a different, accurately drawn, and labeled type.

- **I Went Walking,** Sue Williams, Julie Vivas (illus.). A little girl collects a trail of animals on her walk. Simple text, simple pictures, great for babies who love animals.

- **Miss Spider's Tea Party,** David Kirk. (And the companion board book *Miss Spider's Tea Party: The Counting Book*, David Kirk.) Vivid, detailed illustrations of a spider looking for playmates. Both are excellent, by far the best in this series.

- **Pete's a Pizza,** William Steig. Parents knead their cranky kid into pizza dough, sprinkle him with "toppings," and chase him around the house to "bake" and "eat" him—and turn him from grumpy to giggling in the process. Start reading it to your baby and you'll be tossing your own grumpy toddler pizza before you know it.

- **Good Night, Gorilla,** Peggy Rathmann. The gorilla in this picture book wants to go home with the zookeeper, and he wants all his friends to come too. Any baby who wants to sleep in Mama and Daddy's bed will identify. A nice simple story that baby will quickly want to "read" to herself.

- **Hug,** Jez Alborough. Beautiful, detailed drawings and a single word tell the jungle version of lost in the grocery store.

- **I Stink!,** Kate McMullan, Jim McMullan (illus.). This is a crashing, banging, disgusting, fascinating, and highly onomatopoeic tale of a city garbage truck making its rounds.

- **Olivia,** Ian Falconer. Olivia the pig totes around her cat, takes care of her brother, and wears out her mother, all in black and white accented in red.

- **Dinosaur Binket,** Sandra Boynton. Dinosaur can't go to sleep without his binket.

- **Silly Sally,** Audrey Wood. Silly Sally, a bouncy, fairy-tale-like creature, goes to town, walking backwards upside down, with a pack of upside-down animals trailing behind her.

- **Fireman Small,** Wong Herbert Yee. Fireman Small (who is indeed small) comes to the rhyming rescue of a town full of animals.

- **Everywhere Babies,** Susan Meyers, Marla Frazee (illus.). Babies are everywhere and are shown at their most babyesque selves. Charming and witty and all-inclusive, showing every kind of family.

- **Max's First Word,** Rosemary Wells. Max's first word isn't what Ruby was expecting.

- **Gossie,** Oliver Dunrea. Gossie's red boots are missing. When he finds them, he finds an unexpected friend. Clean, bright, and simple line pictures in a baby-hand sized book.

- ***Moonbear's Shadow,*** **Frank Asch.** Moonbear tries to rid himself of his shadow in a host of silly ways. With oddly flat outlined illustrations in rich colors.

- ***Have You Seen My Cat?*** **Eric Carle.** Well, have you? Plenty of No's, until she turns up.

- ***Noisy Nora,*** **Rosemary Wells.** Being a mouse in the middle isn't easy. Nora triumphs with a wonderful technique that goes from noisy to silent.

Ages and Stages:
Simple Suggestions and Starting Stories

Newborn	<ul><li>Look for postcards (like the freebies marketing companies put near bathrooms in restaurants and bookstores) that your baby might like and carry them around with you so that she always has something new to gaze at.</li><li>Prop open books next to her on the changing table, or tape new images to the wall next to her (or the ceiling, if that's possible).</li><li>Recite a few simple nursery rhymes or make up nonsense rhymes to see if they get a smile.</li></ul>
Heads Up	<ul><li>Books offer a great incentive to lift the head during "tummy time." Put a soft one down flat for a younger baby and arrange some open board books for the baby who can lift her head, and maybe stretch out an arm to topple them.</li></ul>

Sitting	• Substitute baby's name for names in books. • Try bringing the world into a book, offering a leaf with a picture of a tree, or a real apple (to hold and smell) to add to an apple illustration. • He should be able to "lift the flap," so try a few of those. Pass them around among friends if you can, to add variety but avoid purchasing too many, as these have a limited life span. • Play "book peek-a-boo." Use your hand to cover and reveal the thing on the page. It's a big hit.
Crawling/Creeping	• Pass the books back and forth before you read, saying, "Thank you!" • Snap the books open and shut, saying, "Hello! Goodbye!"
Cruising/Walking	• Try loading some books into a push-wagon for delivery into the next room. • Now is a great time for books with handles, or those little sets of books that come in a cardboard "suitcase."
Talking (a few words)	• "Read" a toy catalog or a kids' clothing catalog (we're sure your mailbox is full of them). This won't work so well once he realizes those are things you can HAVE, so try it now.

Talking More	• Can she start learning the names of a few favorite books? Make sure you're reading the title, too, so she can start learning how to ask for it.
Running (but not talking much)	• Try playing "hide and seek" with a book, then reading it once it's found. • Read at mealtime when you have a "captive audience." Offer a book to look at when he's waiting for his lunch, or (and) read to him while he's eating.
Talking ALL THE TIME!	• Try getting a new book and seeing if he can "read" you the story from the pictures. • You're allowed to ignore "Why?" and "What's that?" and "What happened?" after you've answered them three times on a single page. • Try to set aside a time for reading together, TO YOUR-SELVES. You get a book, he gets a book, and you curl up and read. Expect this to last about thirty seconds at this point…but hopefully, you're starting a habit!

Chapter Three:
Baby Lit Crit:
Choosing the Best Books
for *Your* Baby or Toddler

The acquisition of books is inevitable. Gifts, purchases, and hand-me-downs will accumulate until you're tripping over *Pots and Pans* on your way to the kitchen sink. But you and your child will want to choose some (if not most) of the books you share. Since he's not exactly a discerning shopper (most browsing toddlers will go straight for books they already have), you're going to have to choose for him. How to choose? You'll want to:

- Spot your child's tastes—and choose accordingly
- Stick to what's right for your family
- Search out great libraries and booksellers
- Start a library that will grow with you and your baby!

Why Does He Like This Book Better Than That Book?

Starting from very early on, babies have distinct tastes; in food, in colors, in activities, and in books. A familiar book may be soothing, but once he can turn his little head away or push at your hand, you're going to know if he likes something new. Granted, you're screening his choices simply by virtue of being the reader and the chooser at this point—but will he like what you choose?

Remember, the artwork is more than half of the book to your baby. He's the reader of the pictures, after all, and the art is very important to his preferences. Very young babies almost all respond to high contrast images, such as black and white or with just one or two strongly dominant colors. Babies all like pictures of other babies. (Who doesn't?) Babies who say just one or two words will generally like books with those words or objects in them. Many babies at around a year old go through a phase of being very excited about the moon. Any book where you can point out the moon, like *Harold and the Purple Crayon* or *Goodnight, Gorilla,* may thrill him. That's where it ends. Beyond that, there aren't many universals among baby book preferences. What you need is help figuring out what your baby does and doesn't like—and here it is.

The Completely Not Foolproof Method of Selecting Books for YOUR Baby or Toddler

Start by putting together a pile of the books he does like. Are there any similarities? Go beyond the fact that they're all about bears, or they all rhyme. This is a zen process—the key word is "notice." Put aside your preconceptions about what the books are "about" and notice the things your baby notices. Be sure to focus on the art as well as the words.

- Are all the pictures very busy, or are they simple?
- How many images are there on each page?
- Is there more than one line of text per page?
- Are the settings familiar or new, and are they drawn in detail or sketched in very simply?
- Do all the characters have dots for eyes?
- Are the characters all animals, or all human?
- Do the pictures have many colors, or only a few?
- Is there a lot of white on the page, or is it all filled in with art?
- Are the pictures drawings or photographs?
- Is the rhythm fast or slow?
- Does the narrative neatly resolve a problem, or simply recount a story?
- Do the characters talk?
- Does anything else strike you as you look at all the artwork spread out together, no matter how weird it may seem?

The answers to these questions should help you to put together a pretty good list of requirements. As you move your baby into different books—more advanced, longer, or just new to her—you might try changing just one or two elements rather than all of them. For example, the book might have more text, but still have very simple pictures and few colors. Or it might have wild illustrations with very detailed backgrounds and almost no words at all.

Wild and Colorful Books for Baby

- **A Rainbow All Around Me,** Sandra Pinkney, Myles Pinkney (illus.). Vivid photographs of colorful children's faces and clothing.

- **Of Colors and Things,** Tana Hoban. Hoban captures photos of bright, familiar objects worth noticing. (Also *Red, Blue, Yellow Shoe.*)

- **Daddy Kisses,** Anne Gutman, Georg Hallensleben (illus.). Rich, soft colors fill foregrounds and backgrounds of the pictures, showing daddy animals loving their little ones.

- **Run, Mouse, Run!,** Peter Horacek. Graphic, easy to understand illustrations take the mouse on a gallop through a vivid kitchen background.

- **Bunny's First Snowflake,** Monica Wellington. Bright, two-dimensional illustrations filled with detail help children follow the bunny as animals prepare for winter.

A Few More Generalizations (That May Help)

- Very active or very sensitive babies (often one and the same) may be overwhelmed if there are too many things on the page, whereas a very calm baby may be pleasantly stimulated by detailed artwork.

- Unless (until) your baby is very verbal, avoid books where there are ideas in the text that aren't pictured on the page. For example, in *Bedtime for Frances*, Frances "started to think about tigers. She thought about big tigers and little tigers.... " There are no tigers pictured; in fact, the story isn't about tigers at all, and yet she thinks about them for about five lines of text. Generally, these are books to save for an older toddler or preschooler.

- Don't overlook the obvious—if he likes moose, get *If You Give a Moose a Muffin*.
- If your child likes one book by an author or illustrator, then try other books by the same—but don't count on it. Your son may like that book because of the picture of the balloon on page three, not because of the quality of the writing or the art.
- Repetition, repetition, repetition. Repetition holds kids during longer narratives, like *Green Eggs and Ham* (that, the fabulous illustrations, and the fact that Dr. Seuss seems to have had a direct line into the mind of small children. But repetition helps.)
- Keep it short!
- Keep trying. The pictures that were too much for your son at nine months may delight him at eighteen months—opening up a whole new world of busily illustrated books you'd been avoiding. It's a good idea to go through this exercise pretty regularly, even if all you're doing is a mental review of the shelves or of last night's reading as you enter the library.
- Use what you've learned to add variety. If he likes books about bunnies, that doesn't mean you need to go out and buy six more board books about bunnies.

Remember, your baby isn't interested in the newest books, or the most popular. You will undoubtedly find, as he gets older, that he has a favorite book that not one of your friends has ever heard of, that appeared in print for a few months when he was born and then sank into (undeserved) obscurity. Or you may realize that the bunny characters he seems to love so much have achieved such popularity that they are about to become a TV show—which may take away some of the charm for you, but not for your baby. He has his own inscrutable reasons for liking what he likes. Your job is just to decipher them enough to help him find more and more likeable books.

Five Simple, Clean Books for Baby Purists

1. **Spot Goes to the Park,** Eric Hill. Irresistibly bright and immediately accessible for all children. Also available as *Spot Va Al Parque* in Spanish, and in many other languages.

2. **Brown Bear, Brown Bear, What Do You See?,** Bill Martin Jr., Eric Carle (illus.). Brown bear shares a rhythmic word parade with red bird, yellow duck, and blue (!) horse. Also available as *Oso Pardo, Oso Pardo, ¿Qué Ves Ahí?* in Spanish.

3. **I Like It When...,** Mary Murphy. Simple, vivid and excellent activities to share with your toddler.

4. **My Car,** Byron Barton. Simple, bright, bold, and informative about Sam and his beloved car.

5. **Whose Tail?,** Sam Lloyd. Bright, colorful but simple pictures of a chain of animals pulling tails.

Picking Books for Picky Toddlers and Twos

Things get a little easier with a toddler, and easier still as your child becomes a more articulate two-year-old. While sometimes still inscrutable, the choices become a little less opaque. If he calls a book "Doggie Book," then he probably likes it because of the dog, which helps when it comes to choosing new books—more doggie books? Additional animal books?

TRIP TIP: Don't buy a bunch of new books for a young child right before a trip, even if they are about beloved characters or you're really convinced they'll be hits. For the under-three crowd, novelty is good only in limited doses—and the novelty of an airplane, or a new place to sleep, means that the bedtime books, in particular, must stay the same.

Once your child is enjoying a storybook or two, or using two word sentences, it's time to stop buying stuff that's too easy. You won't get much use out of it. Word books are still good, as are counting and alphabet books, but look for them to have more complexity. Choose books with lots of objects to identify on a page, like *Sam's Big Book of Words* by Yves Got. With counting books, try to find those with a story in the counting, like *Ten, Nine, Eight* by Molly Bang, or that go past ten, or have some simple math concepts, like *Cat Count* by Betsy Lewin. Not that you'll find much use for some of this right away, but it's time to start buying books you can grow with.

- Cater to tastes, but don't go overboard. One or two books with identifying pictures of trucks are enough. Try to find books that take the beloved object further—in addition to a book about trucks, try to find one where a truck is driven in the story. If you want a full stack of truck books, hit the library.
- Make reading a new or different book a habit. Try not to repeat the same exact books at bedtime, for example—suggest to your toddler that he pick one (or three) and then you'll pick one.
- Try, try again. Put a book that gets pushed away up on the shelf for a few weeks, or a month, or a year.
- Expand on your toddler's enthusiasms. If he likes a song about whales, try a book about a whale. If he saw a hot air balloon, look for a book with a hot air balloon.

- Now's the time when more of the same will probably be a success—more Max and Ruby, more Charlie and Lola, more Daisy. We're firm believers that while you can have too many toys—so many stuffed animals that no one ever becomes special—you can't have too many books. You read them in groups of at least four, after all—read four books, three times a day, and that's eighty-four books a week. So go ahead, get the whole series if you can manage it. Check out fifteen books from the library. Gorge yourselves.
- DON'T put away the baby books! We've said this before, but it bears repeating—they're comforting. Plus, a really deeply familiar book may be a more satisfying companion in the stroller or the back seat—one she can "read" all by herself.
- Look for books that reflect something your toddler is thinking about or dealing with. Even if she doesn't talk much yet, you know if she's been having trouble sharing or separating. A book could help validate her concerns and ease her difficulties.

Ask your toddler or preschooler why he thinks baby likes a certain book. His insights may surprise you—after all, he's been there a lot more recently than you have!

Can You Take Your Tastes out of the Equation?

Here's a question—are there more books about cats on your baby's shelf, or more about dogs? Bet the answer corresponds with whether you're a cat person or a dog person. We'll also bet you'd never really thought about it. How else are you unconsciously (or consciously) influencing your baby's library? Would you buy *Angelina Ballerina* for your little boy, or *Machines at Work* for your daughter? When you push a book aside, is it the art, or the subject matter, or just that you don't like snakes? Borrowing a few different books from the library could be liberating. Live a little. Your baby may really like cats.

Ten Books that Play to Common Toddler Obsessions

1. **WHALES: *Baby Beluga,*** Raffi, Ashley Wolff (illus.). Watercolor illustrations show the baby whale in the deep blue sea.

2. **HOT AIR BALLOONS: *The Grumpalump,*** Sarah Hayes, Barbara Firth (illus.). A funny cumulative book, as a series of animals investigate a pile of grunting cloth that inflates into a fanciful hot air balloon.

3. **BUGS: *Bugs! Bugs! Bugs!,*** Bob Barner. Bright and beautiful collage illustrations bring bugs to life, from caterpillars to roly-poly bugs, while a few age-appropriate facts and drawings that show each bug at real life size add a little learning.

4. **TRUCKS: *Tough Trucks,*** Tony Mitton, Ant Parker (illus.). Animal truckers drive colorful trucks of all kinds in this descriptive board book.

5. **FISH: *Ten Little Fish,*** Audrey Wood, Bruce Wood (illus.). Bright computer-generated fish disappear, counting down from ten to one, until the last remaining fish meets a mate and has babies, bringing the number, page by page, up to ten again.

6. **TRAINS: *I Love Trains!,*** Philemon Sturges, Shari Halpern (illus.). The young narrator extols his love for the flat, colorful trains that roll by his perch on the hills, naming each car.

7. **MOON: *Moonbeam Bear,*** Rolf Fanger, Ulrike Moltgen (illus.), Marianne Martens (translator). Soft, snuggly-looking Moonbeam Bear loves the moon so much he pulls it out of the sky, and the glowing crescent becomes his friend. Will the moon return to the sky? Will it come back to visit Moonbeam Bear? Of course.

8. **DINOSAURS: *Dinosaur Roar!,*** Paul and Henrietta Stickland. Cheerful watercolor dinosaurs portray opposites in brief rhyming couplets on their way to lunch.

9. **FIREFIGHTERS: *Fire Truck,*** Peter Sís. A little boy who loves to play and dream about fire trucks wakes up one day with wheels and flashing lights and gets to spend the morning as a fire truck. A perfect depiction of every little child who's ever announced "I'm not a baby, I'm a truck. "

10. **BALLERINAS: *Ballerina!,*** Peter Sís. A very simple book about a plump and appealing little line drawing of a girl who loves to dance.

Your Child's Choices: Living with *Supercat*

KJ lived with Supercat for months. *Supercat to the Rescue,* to be precise—a truly adorable first comic book for a toddler, with a sturdy rectangular shape perfect for holding open and turning pages. For what seemed like an interminable period when Sam was three, it became his absolute favorite—the one book he would always choose above any other.

Your child will have favorites, and these will be the books you read over and over again. Sometimes you can hide a book you don't like before it becomes a favorite, but other times, you won't have the heart or the opportunity. You may not realize it wouldn't be your choice until it's too late, or you may actually think the book is cute, the first thirty times. And there you'll be, exclaiming "Meowie Wowie!" into eternity. Inevitably, you're going to ask yourself: Why? What are you getting out of my reading this book over and over again? Why this one? Unfortunately, any book your child wants to hear at every single reading session is going to become boring to you, no matter how much you liked it in the first place. So, why? Why? WHY?

Quite simply, nearly every child does this at some point or another. Susan's son Ben, starting at twenty months, made her read *The Story of Ferdinand* repeatedly for days and weeks on end. One particular passage seemed to resonate with Ben. When Ferdinand's mother showed her concern about his un-bullish ways, Ferdinand reassured her. "His mother saw that he was not lonesome, and because she was an understanding mother, even though she was a cow, she let him just sit there and be happy. " Every time Susan read this, Ben would

Zoe's top ten

We've been reading to Zoe (twenty-three months) since she came home from the hospital. We read all the way through Harry Potter before she could sit up. She seems to enjoy reading—often saying, "I want book," or, "I read!" We always read at bedtime and then usually a book or two once or twice during the day. Sometimes she sits down with a book and just pages through it as if reading by herself. I like to read to her while she eats her lunch because she is really attentive and participatory (and a captive audience in her high chair!). Some of our favorite books are:

1. Corduroy
2. Miss Spider's Tea Party
3. Go, Dog. Go!
4. One Fish, Two Fish, Red Fish, Blue Fish
5. One Hungry Monster
6. Max Cleans Up
7. Where the Wild Things Are
8. Elmo Loves You
9. Hush Little Baby
10. I Love Trains!

By the way, I HATE The Rainbow Fish!!! Although some say its premise is about sharing, I think the message is more about buying friendship and not appreciating the fact that each fish is different and uniquely beautiful in its own way. It also seems to encourage the concept that in order to be viewed as "good/nice" you have to give away that which is most precious to you. It seems very socialist in concept. —Melissa

remove his thumb or bottle from his mouth and say, firmly, "Good!" Susan knew he identified with Ferdinand and was doing his best to get her to be as understanding as Mrs. Cow.

Why are you rereading your book noir over and over again? There are several possible answers. Your child may really need to hear this story (and may need you to hear it) like Ben with Ferdinand. Part of the reason for Sam's fixation on Supercat turned out to be that Supercat brings Bitsy a comforting nightlight, and Sam wanted one, too. Or it may be just pure pleasure in the words, the sentence structure, the language, the pictures, the colors, or even the shape of the book.

Once he can understand the suggestion, have your toddler choose a book to take along every time you go out. You'll be starting a habit that will help him get through countless car rides, long waits, and tedious (to him) adult chats. It will serve you both well!

It's also true that if you're a book lover, you know that you never want a really good book to end. Your baby doesn't, either. He's still learning about books. It's comforting that they really are the same, every single time. Today, Supercat will always bring the nightlight. Tomorrow, Charlotte will always die in the end—but Wilbur will never become bacon. Or maybe he just wants to hear it again because you didn't linger long enough on the page with the fireflies, or really adequately perform the Boo Boo dance. Even if you did, "read it again" assures that you will once again perform. For once, he's in control (at least until you balk). And he knows what will happen next. For a baby or a toddler, that's big. You're just going to have to learn to live with it, and even try to learn to love it. And make sure the babysitter reads it a few hundred times, too.

Five Books that Trigger, "Again! Again!" Again and Again

1. **Belly Button Book,** Sandra Boynton. One of Boynton's trademark verse chants features hippos and their beloved belly buttons.

2. **The Little Engine That Could,** Watty Piper. Something about the already repetitive text of this classic inspires kids to ask for it again and again. "I think I can. I think I can."

3. **Is Your Mama a Llama?,** Deborah Guarino, Steven Kellogg (illus.). Clever rhymes and riddles keep kids turning the pages, then starting all over again.

4. **One Fish, Two Fish, Red Fish, Blue Fish,** Dr. Seuss. Will you or your baby memorize it first?

5. **Who Said Moo?,** Harriet Ziefert, Simms Taback (illus.). Lift the flaps to discover who answered Rooster's morning crow, then to make sure the answer never changes. (Also *Where Is My Baby?*)

And the Moral of the Story Is...

Lots of baby books have messages about sharing and friendship and the like. Messages that, surprisingly enough, you may dislike. *The Rainbow Fish* is a book that engenders strong reactions. Is it about sharing, or buying popularity at the price of individuality? *The Runaway Bunny* is another "controversial" book—is the mama bunny smothering her little one, or making him feel safe and protected?

If you're reading along and suddenly find you don't like the turn the story's taken, it's fine to voice your emotion—"Hey, I don't think that's what she should have done at all!" You're hoping to pass your values on, after all—there's no time like now for opening the discussion, whether your baby can talk back or not!

"Jack, twenty months, is such an active kid, it really is magic the way he can be 'stilled' by a book. Without question it is my favorite thing when he comes over with one he has selected, hands it to me, and commands 'read' as he plops himself into my lap (usually with the pronouncement 'sit down'). The books have become part of his emotional life, helping him to sort out new feelings. The Runaway Bunny (by Margaret Wise Brown) is an all-time favorite. . . an obsession, really. I wasn't sure how I felt about the storyline—the mother's practice of following the bunny wherever he goes may be somehow comforting to the toddler who is ambivalent about his independence, but to me it borders on stalking ('If you become a sailboat and sail away from me, I'll become the wind and blow you where I want you to go.')! But Jack loves it. When still a new walker just beginning to quicken his pace to a run, he'd speed down the hallway yelling, 'Run away, run away.' Then soon after, it seeped into our morning routine, which had been for me to bring him milk that he would drink in his crib, allowing me another ten minutes or so of rest. One morning he began to cry when I left the room. When I rushed back to ask him what was wrong he said desperately, 'Mommy go away,' and I knew that he meant he felt abandoned—unlike the stalker bunny mommy, I had left." —Kate

One More Choice: Hardcover, Paperback, Board Book?

Board books are wonderful for babies who rip pages, for moms with tired arms, and for throwing into the bag with all the other supplies. Some books—especially those designed for very little babies, like baby face pictures and naming books—only come in this format, and it's likely to be all you use from the time baby starts grabbing until she's ready to move on to longer stories. When buying a book that's available in several formats, it's a good idea to check to see whether the board book omits anything. The board book for *Chicka Chicka Boom Boom* cuts off the second half, leaving out half the fun. Other books may combine text from two pages onto one and drop an illustration.

Some board books that stem from popular series, like Olivia and Curious George, are not really books by the author at all—they're the author's original illustrations with simple, usually non-narrative text, like counting or opposite books. Some of these can be very good (*Miss Spider's Tea Party: The Counting Book* is a wonderful example that manages to retain the spirit of the original). Others are definitely riding on the strength of the franchise. Generally, if you know the author's dead, the spin-off books based on his or her work may also be lifeless.

Once your baby has really started to enjoy the ritual of reading (you'll know because you'll find yourself actually finishing the majority of books you start), it's probably time to stop purchasing board books. Paperbacks are often cheaper and just as beautifully illustrated as board books and hardcovers, and they're wonderfully light for travel. Hardcover books, though, have a magic of their own—a smell and a feel that can create a sensory memory even apart from the pictures and the story—and they're likely to stand up to more wear. (But don't forget to stock up on tape.)

Where to Get Them, Where to Keep Them

We love all bookstores. We love our local independent bookstores; labors of love, each and every one. We support them with visits and dollars. We love Barnes & Noble and the other superstores, too, where we can surround ourselves with books and booklovers and have constant access to coffee and treats. But the big stores can be a problem if you've got a baby in tow—they're overwhelming if you need to get in and out quickly, and the staff may or may not be knowledgeable about children's books. Plus, paying full price for every book you buy gets expensive. So here's a quick run down on what else is out there and why you might want to give it a try.

Look for a bookstore with a basket of toys and a small enough kids' area that you can keep one eye on a mobile baby or toddler as you browse, and you'll be able to preview the books but still make the bookstore a family outing. Beware the toddler making a break for the cookie case in the coffee shop!

Libraries

It's amazing how many new moms forget the library entirely, yet there's no better way to taste-test books and feed your hunger for something new. Even the smallest community libraries usually have a children's room with a specially trained children's librarian, and she won't be limited to books that are currently in print. If there's a problem with even the most knowledgeable bookstore staffer, it's that she's probably slightly biased towards the newer books because she may be more familiar with them. Librarians can lead you to authors and books you might never find otherwise.

Small Bookstores

If you have a local bookstore specializing in children's books or an independent bookseller with a large children's section, use and support it. It's a great resource. The owners and staff of these stores devote a considerable amount of time to all forms of children's literature, and they'll know what you mean when you request a book about farm animals with simple illustrations and no more than one line of text per page.

Used Bookstores, Secondhand Shops, Garage Sales

Book conditions vary greatly, and you'll probably find some that are practically new. Since you hope they'll become worn with use, why shouldn't the books start out a little tattered?

Discount Stores

TJ Maxx and similar stores receive regular shipments of overstocked children's books. They can have some wonderful deals on books, particularly if you ask when they expect to receive new shipments and plan accordingly. Stores like Target or Wal-Mart may also offer a small discount on current titles.

Street Vendors

In major cities, you'll find street vendors with tables full of books you've never heard of, from publishers you've never seen before. These vendors are a great source for naming books, alphabet books, or coloring books, and those laminated placemats with educational facts and such on them. (If you do find a vendor selling one or two copies of a popular title, unused, or selling books you recognize from the bookstore, beware. The New York City Police Department warns that these books are often stolen or off the grey market. You do want to support the authors, illustrators, and publishers who have brought your family so much pleasure!)

Online Shopping

So convenient, but with one problem—unless you're looking for specific titles, it's hard to tell what you're getting. Amazon.com offers a "look inside" feature with some books, but not all, and without that you won't be able to see the illustrations or judge the amount of text on the page. Many sites include reader (parent) reviews, which can be helpful, and Amazon also has a fun feature called "listmania" that allows users to create lists like "Best Bedtime Books for Toddlers." You may find shopping easier at a smaller site like www.commonreader.com, which offers a "carefully chosen and happily personal selection." The site may not be as easy to use, but a prescreened selection can be a little less daunting if it seems like you share a basic philosophy. Because those sites tend to be owner-run (the online equivalent to an independent bookstore), you can even call with questions. Many have catalogs as well.

Online Auctions

If you're in the market for a lot of books, and you don't mind sorting through them once you've got them, try eBay or one of the other auction sites. Parents trying to make room for older kids box the baby books up and sell them in lots. Some will list every title they're selling, others just a select few. A box of twenty books may go for as little as $12. Don't forget that shipping is added on after the bidding stops. It's not a bargain if you find yourself paying $5 or $10 more in shipping costs!

Shelves, Baskets, and Piles

Your baby wants to be able to get to her books at all times, for easy chewing, perusing, and reading with her grown-ups. You want them neat and out-of-the-way. It's time for a compromise—after all, if she can't get to the books, how will she be able to read them, play with them, or use them for building blocks? For the most part, traditional book storage won't work well. If her books are lined up tightly on the shelf with only their spines showing, she won't be able to pick which one she wants or pull it out. You need a solution that allows her easy access but allows you to get to her crib without stepping on *The Foot Book*.

For starters, try not to keep the books all in one place. You want to be able to read at any time of the day without having to go to one specific location, and you want the constant presence of books to suggest reading activities to both of you. Different rooms may call for different solutions. You might have room for a special children's bookshelf that allows the books to be displayed with their covers showing in the nursery or playroom, and for other rooms you might consider baskets, boxes, or magazine racks. All are more easily accessible for baby than a regular shelf. If you are using shelves, try stacking the books up or keeping the shelves loose so that it's easy to pull them out (and keep in mind that pulling them out may be the part your baby likes best!).

IRRESISTIBLE AUTHOR ROSEMARY WELLS

Rosemary Wells's contribution to the world of books for very young children is incalculable. We all see ourselves and our children in her Max and Ruby series of sibling rivalries, or Noisy Nora's plight as the middle child, or the feisty Tulip who triumphantly messes up her nemesis Benjamin. Ms. Wells has an immediately recognizable aesthetic and seems to have accurately remembered childhood's trials perfectly. Although her characters are little animals (kittens, bunnies, and woodchuck-like dogs) they burst with human life and foibles.

Can't Put Them Down Storybooks
Blockbuster Fiction for the Younger Set

No library is complete without books that tell a story, but many babies who are just starting to sit still and really participate in the reading aren't ready for much of a narrative. They need very short stories. Plot development is not that important to them. You may even find that your more verbal or more patient baby is really ready for some longer tales—but many of the beautiful hardcovers in the store have a whole paragraph of text on each page. That's too much for most babies and toddlers. We've provided some starter storybooks that can ease your baby gently into longer listening times. Older toddlers may be ready for longer stories, and we've included our favorites here, too.

- *Angus and the Cat,* Marjorie Flack. Angus the dog accepts a cat into his home, with simple pictures, few colors, and a fun twist told only in the illustrations.

- *Bark, George,* Jules Feiffer. Mama dog takes her puppy, George, to the vet to see why he can't bark. Great simple illustrations.

- *Come Along, Daisy!,* Jane Simmons. A familiar tale for any walker who's lagged behind Mama amid the world's many distractions.

- *Duck on a Bike,* David Shannon. The title says it all. All the farm animals eventually appear on bikes. Good for the toddler with a new tricycle or seat on Dad's bike.

- *Giggle, Giggle, Quack,* Doreen Cronin, Betsy Lewin (illus.). A little easier to understand for a toddler than this author's other popular book, *Click Clack Moo*. A duck types messages from the barn.

- *Have You Seen My Duckling?,* Nancy Tafuri. The "lost" duckling can be seen hiding on each page as the mother queries the other animals around the pond.

- *Mr. Gumpy's Outing,* John Burningham. A cumulative book about farm animals on a raft and the inevitable disaster, which is handled quite calmly. Pencil drawings.

Longer Stories

- *The Great Gracie Chase,* Cynthia Rylant, Mark Teague (illus.). Gracie the dog runs away accidentally and finds herself being chased by the whole town. Lots of repetition and a surprise ending.

- *The Story of Ferdinand,* Munro Leaf, Robert Lawson (illus.). Susan's son Ben's favorite book as a toddler. Black and white illustrations. A bull stays true to himself—even if he's not exactly the bull anyone expected.

- *Rolie Polie Olie,* William Joyce. With colorful, computer-generated illustrations and a playful family of round-headed aliens, *Rolie Polie Olie* tells the story of rambunctious boy Olie, whose day includes the Rolie Polie Rumba Dance ("always done in underpants"), a sibling spat, and bedtime forgiveness.

- *Beatrice Doesn't Want To,* Laura Nate Numeroff, Lynn Munsinger (illus.). Beatrice, a visibly stubborn pencil-and-ink canine little sister, doesn't want to do anything that might make it easier for Henry to take care of her, including a visit to the library. But once she gets there, she's so captivated by storytime that she doesn't want to leave.

- *Sheep in a Jeep,* Nancy E. Shaw, Margot Apple (illus.). Clever rhymes in every line. Sheep make mistakes but clean up their messes.

- *Green Eggs and Ham and The Cat in the Hat,* Dr. Seuss. Rhyming story classics suitable for all ages.

- *Hiding Hoover,* Elise Broach, Laura Huliska-Beith (illus.). When Daddy says they can't have a pet, two clever children adopt a dragon and hide him right under Daddy's nose (or do they?). Color-filled, extravagant illustrations.

- *The Fantastic Mr. Wani,* Kanako Usui. Alligator Mr. Wani causes all sorts of trouble among his simply drawn animal friends just trying to get to a party.

- **Sakes Alive! A Cattle Drive!,** Karma Wilson, Karla Firehammer (illus.). When a pair of cows decide to take the car for a spin, things go from disaster to unexpected success.

- **Cold Little Duck, Duck, Duck,** Lisa Westberg Peters, Sam Williams (illus.). Baby Duck arrives too soon for spring but soon dreams a glorious spring into being for all the animals.

- **Little Bunny on the Move,** Peter McCarty. Soft, luminous watercolors in a nearly black and white palette follow Little Bunny as he resists all other destinations and heads for home.

- **Hop, Jump,** Ellen Stoll Walsh. Two dimensional frogs in remarkable detail against a background of mostly clean white space at first resist the one who, tired of all this hopping, encourages them to dance, but soon all but one join in. That's okay, because there's room for both dancing and hopping in this world.

- **Guji Guji,** Chih-Yuan Chen. A crocodile hatches amidst a brood of ducklings, but no matter how different he grows, he's loved by his mama duck and stays true to his family.

- **Never, Ever Shout in a Zoo,** Karma Wilson, Doug Cushman (illus.). Wild and mischievous animals take over when the narrator's advice is ignored in a festive, brightly colored romp of consequences.

- **How to Catch a Star,** Oliver Jeffers. Flat, whimsical images show a boy sitting on a beach, waiting for the stars to drop, to no avail…until a starfish washes ashore.

- **Zoom! Zoom! Zoom! I'm Off to the Moon!,** Dan Yaccarino. Simple artwork in a broad palette of colors illustrates a boy's trip to the moon from takeoff to landing.

Ages and Stages:
What to Look for in a Book at Every Stage

Newborn	• Starkly contrasting images in black and white or primary colors are most likely to catch an infant's attention. If he's interested, give him plenty of time to look.
Heads Up	• Cloth and rubber books are great for babies just gaining more control over their bodies. Look for the simplest and brightest.
Sitting	• Photographed or drawn pictures of baby faces, ideally nice big ones, look like familiar friends.
Crawling/Creeping	• In addition to the baby pictures, simple lift-the-flaps are wonderful for babies practicing using their hands.
Cruising/Walking	• Newly minted toddlers love silly rhymes and animal sounds.
Talking (a few words)	• Look for any book with those first words in it. Nothing's more exciting than a chance to point and yell, "Dog!"
Talking More	• Nursery rhymes can allow a child who's getting more verbal to fill in the blanks with the "punch rhyme."
Running (but not talking much)	• Books with lots of action sounds or songs set to music can provide an opportunity to move around while still enjoying the reading.
Talking ALL THE TIME!	• Get out those story books and talk about what happens, or turn the tables with a wordless book he can "read" to you.

Chapter Four:
It's All in the Telling: Reading Aloud, Making It Up, and Desperately Seeking Cinderella

Before there were picture books, there were stories. Stories with morals, stories to explain why the rains came and the sun rose, stories about the old days, when every caveman had to walk ten miles (uphill, both ways) to bring back fire to his people. We still tell stories today, for entertainment and for passing on memories and family legends.

Most of us can handle telling the story of the time Uncle Jim's pants caught on fire to a (hopefully) new audience. But storytelling seems to take on a new meaning when you add babies and children to the mix. You might start with telling the baby what's happening as it unfolds: who's there, what comes next in the diaper change, how wonderful life is with her in your world. When (and if) you run out of things to talk about, reach for a book.

Suddenly, you're reading out loud, talking your way through picture books, and trying to remember fairy tales. It's a little daunting. Luckily, you can start out with the most undemanding of audiences—newborns—and work your way up. You can also start with the easy stuff, reading aloud from picture books, where characters, story, and pictures are all before you and your only job is to bring them to life. Telling stories from wordless picture books, relating fairy tales, and making up your own stuff can come a little later. By the time your baby is really listening to the stories you tell, you'll be telling them with ease.

What's So Important about a Story?

At their best, simple early storybooks tap into the emotional and imaginative experience of childhood for both the baby and the reader. The baby sees and hears that there is an arc to experience; that most things—days, meals, diaper changes, stories—have a beginning, a middle, and an end; an introduction, a crisis, and a resolution. The adult is put in touch with childhood feelings in a fresh, surprising way. Even the smallest readers have a distinct preference for stories at reading time. Naming books are more like games for gaining mastery of vocabulary; stories are for reading.

In reading a story to a baby, a toddler, or a preschooler, there is a physical closeness, a joining together as one. It is difficult for others to interrupt; often, the power of storytelling encourages those outside the immediate circle to sit and listen, too. The narrative pulls everyone in together. The protagonists in the very best stories for young children have a dilemma that speaks not just to the concerns of the small child but to some universal, larger concern for us all. Earlier in the book Susan talked about her son Ben's fascination with Ferdinand. Ferdinand is the classic outsider—seemingly powerless, but able, in the end, to remain true to himself and resist the powerful lure of others' expectations. The baby rejoices in Ferdinand's return to home, mother, flowers, and serenity. The adult may value Ferdinand's ability to embrace being different (particularly since that difference takes a non-violent form) and his trust that his mother will still love him, regardless of what kind of bull he is.

Stories for very young babies don't have to have powerful messages, even though some of them do. What's important is a main character. The baby will begin to identify with and root for him even if he's an elephant like Babar or a baby bull like Ferdinand. Each of these stories is a baby's introduction to one of the main pleasures of reading—the comforting resolution that is almost always to be found at the end of a children's story. Everyone lives happily ever after.

Reading Stories Aloud: The Basics for Grown-Ups

The stories may be brilliant, but not everyone finds conveying them easy. It's normal and fair to feel awkward about reading aloud, even to the least demanding of audiences. After all, until you had a baby, the last time you read aloud was probably in an English classroom full of your peers, alternately critical, bored, or inattentive. Your baby will be none of those things. She'll be delighted, enchanted, and enthralled, however you do it. Even if you mispronounce the name "Hermione" every single time, she's going to think that's the perfect way to read. If others in the room listening—your partner, your spouse, your mother—make you feel self-conscious, read with just your baby until you feel more comfortable.

Library Storytimes

Many libraries offer "storytimes" for designated age groups. There is a lively trend to offer programs to very young babies. The caregivers have a wonderful time too. Some programs are very organized, with a quiet time for reading and usually some play time after. Others are more of a free-for-all, with a higher tolerance for kids running up to see Olivia or away to demonstrate a few marching moves. Try out a few in your community and see which type suits your baby best.

You have years of reading aloud ahead and plenty of time to develop your own style. A few tips follow, but our most important advice is to just grab a book and go. The rest will come naturally with a very little bit of practice.

Remember, the words and the text are just part of the reading experience for your baby. While you read the words, she's reading the artwork. Without the pictures, there would be no book at all! You are the announcer, the conduit, the phone line, the television set—the entrée into the world of the book. But while you're reading aloud, the book is the world.

Tone and Volume

Obviously, you can read loudly in the middle of the afternoon and softly at night. Even better, you can crescendo when the Cat brings in Thing One and Thing Two and whisper in shock when mother approaches and the mess is yet to be cleared up. You can also take a tone that's appropriate for the story—excited and happy, yes, for dancing hippos and shopping sheep, but sympathetic and calm for the monkey who's lost his mother and needs a hug, or the owl babies who await their mother's return. You are entering into the emotional world of the book.

Great Starter Read-Alouds No One Can Resist

- **The Three Billy Goats Gruff,** Paul Galdone. Three trip-trapping goats outsmart a troll.

- **Five Little Monkeys Jumping on the Bed,** Eileen Christelow. Mama calls the doctor and everybody giggles.

- **A Chair for My Mother,** Vera B. Williams. A story of three generations of women helping each other and what a young girl can do to participate fully. *(Un Sillón para Mi Mamá.)*

- **The Complete Adventures of Peter Rabbit,** Beatrix Potter. A rich source of story telling from one of the first, and one of the enduring best.

- **Frog and Toad Are Friends,** Arnold Lobel. Rewarding stories galore about friends. *(Sapo y Sepo Son Amigos.)*

- **Little Bear,** Else Holmelund Minarik, Maurice Sendak (illus.). Important simple stories about a child-bear and his family.

- **Snuffy,** Dick Bruna. Excellent and concise stories from this internationally renowned story teller for very young children, the author of the Miffy books.

- **The House That Jack Built,** Simms Taback. Taback's house is delightfully full of details with labels, animals, and odors everywhere.

- **Horton Hears a Who!,** Dr. Seuss. It's easy to follow the drama and rhythm of this classic Seuss tale, and even the least comfortable reader will get caught up.

Taking an appropriate emotional tone at certain points of a story helps to teach your child about feelings. Your baby sees you responding empathically to the characters' dilemmas. You help her to understand that the dog is sad because he misses his family, and the owls are anxious as they await their mother's return. Your baby will learn from the characters in the books and their experiences, but you and your voice and tone and facial expressions will always be her barometer and touchstone (and her reminder that, after all, it's only a story in a book).

Animation and Voices

It's up to you—do Max and Ruby have special squeaky voices? Do the animals each have a real (or silly) animal sound? It doesn't matter—some of the best readers aloud modify their voices only slightly for each character, and others have a repertoire that could offer them a lifetime career with Disney studios. Trust us, their kids love them either way. Sometimes a really, really bad imitation of a lion growling is much funnier than the best copy of the real thing. One caveat—if you do a really special and amazing voice or sound once, expect to be doing it again. And again. And again. Possibly for years. Not that that should stop you!

Rhythm, Rhyme, and Repetition

In some books, the rhythm is the very essence of the book. In others, it's more subtle. Once you've found it you'll want to use it. The rhythm shows you where to put the emphasis and even how long to pause between pages. Rhyming words are usually the ones that get emphasized, and once you're putting a little more force on those words, you'll usually find that you're following the rhythm of the book naturally. Trust yourself, and be aided by the writer or poet. These books can lend themselves to bedtime—no matter how lively the story, the rhythm can always be slowed down to sleepytime levels.

Like advertising jingles, baby books are repetitious to better stick in your mind. Repetition focuses the mind by creating patterns. We get the message and learn to predict what's coming next. In reading aloud, repetition of words and phrases gives you the opportunity to be creative. You can make a joke by getting it wrong or add your child's name to a list.

> *"My daughter's only seven weeks old, and she's had a terrible time with infant stomach cramps. I just read her a couple of chapters of Winnie the Pooh, and she listened. She looked at the pictures. She loved the sound of my voice. And it went on like that for more than twenty minutes! Quite frankly, she could have gone on for longer, but I quit because I got tired. I was amazed. "* —Rita

Wordless Books

Here's the thing about wordless books: the whole story is in the pictures. These books don't need words. Here's the thing about most parents: we can't read a wordless book without talking. We see a story in pictures and we talk about it.

Reading begins with observing. Many picture books, even those with plenty of words, also tell their story in the pictures. Wordless books (by which we mean pure wordless books like *First Snow* or books like *Good Night, Gorilla* or *Oink* that may have a word or two) can be huge fun. They put you and your baby on the same page, inviting you both to enter into the story visually.

Wordless books also make reading simple. The illustrations are loaded with narrative information, so a story naturally moves along with dramas and development.

Even insecure readers or non-English speaking parents will surprise themselves that they can tell a story just by saying what they notice.

Soon enough a baby will read a wordless book to herself. She develops the ability to interpret what she sees rather than have it interpreted for her through another's words. She begins to comprehend a story line and character interaction, to anticipate what happens next and identify with the character's plight. All these are evident signs of intelligent pre-reading and lead directly to reading.

As children grow into talkers during their second year, wordless books prompt them to tell you what they see, to invent stories, and imagine dialogues. Their renditions are just as valid as yours are. "What do you see?" works equally well for the parent as for the child. "What happens next?" does too. Your version and hers could in fact lead to a lively discussion, a kind of baby book group, fun for you both. See our list of excellent wordless books. You'll be as delighted as your baby. We promise.

Ten Wordless Favorites

1. **Good Dog, Carl,** Alexandra Day. The soft-focus illustrations belay the absurdity and humor of this tale of a babysitting Rottweiler.

2. **Sunshine,** Jan Ormerod. This silent gem follows a very little girl through her day. The companion book *Moonlight* is also a treasure, as it follows the same little one through preparing for bedtime.

3. **Mouse Numbers: A Very First Counting Book,** Jim Arnosky. Simple, framed, and entertaining, we see a mouse leave his zero-shaped burrow entrance, past one toadstool, up and down two hills etc. on a delightful adventure.

4. ***Oink,*** Arthur Geisert. This pink book's illustrations are cleverly amusing. A mother pig has eight piglets full of repeatable and funny oinks. (Oink is the sound a pig makes in English, and German AND Spanish. This book is therefore, according to Mr. Geisert, the only book ever written simultaneously in three languages! The sequel is *Oink, Oink.*)

5. ***Pancakes for Breakfast,*** Tomie dePaola. A farmer and her animals produce every ingredient for a pancake breakfast.

6. ***Shopping Trip,*** Helen Oxenbury. We can all identify with this mother's experiences shopping with her youngster. Almost everything Oxenbury draws is seemingly so simple, yet there's always a palpable emotion.

7. ***10 Minutes till Bedtime,*** Peggy Rathmann. Dad doesn't notice the hamster tourists visiting the little boy hero at bedtime. Every page is full of details that tell the tale in cartoonesque drawings.

8. ***Truck,*** Donald Crews. Like his other books adored by toddlers, this one is bold, clear, colorful, and entertainingly easy to read. The truck encounters lots of weather and real roadside signs and construction as it carries its load of bicycles.

9. ***Four Hungry Kittens,*** Emily Arnold McCully. Plenty of wordless drama about kittens locked in a barn and saved by an alert dog and farmer. (Also *Picnic, First Snow, School.*)

10. ***A Boy, a Dog, a Frog, and a Friend,*** Mercer Mayer. One of the best ever. Through its pictures, it tells the story of a boy and a dog trying to catch a frog. It's fresh, humorous, and full of surprises.

Fairy Tales:
Telling the Stories Everyone Knows (or Thinks They Do!)

When you need a story and you need it fast, it's natural to reach into your mind for a "once upon a time" classic fairy tale. *Goldilocks*, *The Three Little Pigs*, *Little Red Riding Hood*—they seem to reside in all of us, and we see their echoes in endless books and cultural references. If you haven't thought about Little Red for years, you may find she holds a few surprises. What was she doing in the woods again? And wasn't there something about a wolf eating Grandma? What's that about? And now that we come to think of it, where did this come from anyway? Among all the books we've read and stories we've heard, why do these stick with us?

Fairy Tales Connect with a Child's Developmental Stage

Fairy tales imply stories of wonder and enchantment. They also resonate profoundly in an emotionally deep place. In some cases they hit the nail on the head at the time a child is squarely in a developmental phase.

The story of Rumplestiltskin can be a good fit during potty training, a time when many children seem to feel they're struggling with an impossible task. At the root of the story, there is the challenge for a young girl to turn straw into gold. If she accomplishes this amazing feat, she will please her mother, please the father/husband/king character, and become a queen. Why would such an odd tale continue to have universal appeal if it didn't touch something profound and speak to something beyond a child's ability to put into words?

And Then What Happened?
New and Continued Versions of Our Favorite Fairy Tales

- *Goldie and the Three Bears,* Diane Stanley. The eternally picky Goldilocks wanders into the Bears' house while looking for a friend who's "just right."

- *A Chair for Baby Bear,* Kaye Umansky, Chris Fisher (illus.). Baby bear's family sets out to buy him a new chair (since his is broken), but nothing is just right until a gift arrives from Goldilocks.

- *Dusty Locks and the Three Bears,* Susan Lowell, Randy Cecil (illus.). Goldilocks is a grubby little tomboy in this modern version.

- *The Girl Who Spun Gold,* Virginia Hamilton, Leo & Diane Dillon (illus.). An African version of Rumpelstiltskin that highlights the power of storytelling (and names) with gorgeous real gold paintings.

- *Three Cool Kids,* Rebecca Emberley. These three billy goats live in the city and are challenged by a rat.

- *Cinderella,* James Marshall (illus.). As with all of Marshall's quirky artwork, this Cinderella has humor tucked into every crevice. (Also *Goldilocks and the Three Bears, Red Riding Hood,* and *The Three Little Pigs.*)

- *Rumpelstiltskin,* Paul O. Zelinsky. This version delivers a brief story and many elegant two-page spreads. We especially admire the scene of dark night illuminated by the full moon and lamp lights when the queen searches the kingdom for the little man.

- *The Ugly Duckling,* Hans Christian Andersen, Jerry Pinkney (illus.). This version of Hans Christian Andersen's fairy tale is really ducky, and watery.

- **Thumbelina,** Hans Christian Anderson, Brian Pinkney (illus.). A wedding to a mole? Luckily this tiny little creature is rescued by a kind bird who takes her to live happily ever after with the flower people.

- **Rumpelstiltskin,** Paul Galdone. Conrad? Harry? Rumpelstiltskin. In this animated story with excellent artwork, the perspectives and angles tell even more about the angry dwarf.

- **Stone Soup,** Jon J. Muth. Zen monks are involved in this retelling of this trickster tale that celebrates the power of generosity. The drawings are painterly and full of atmosphere.

- **The Three Bears,** Byron Barton. The classic story simplified, with his colorful blocky illustrations.

The story of *Goldilocks and the Three Bears* is a cheerful reversal of something quite scary to a child who feels secure in her family and threatened by outsiders. Just why Goldilocks is lost and wandering near the Bears' house isn't clear, but anyone can see the cozy appeal of the Bears' home, filled with steaming porridge, comfy chairs, and soft beds. It's funny to see the little girl as a threat to the Bears' predictable world, rather than the other way around.

The adventurous appeal of the *Three Little Pigs* speaks to toddlers just able to move away from their secure home base (mother). This is a time when a baby understands that she is really an individual, with her own impulses and the ability to run away and say no. Moving off, however giddy and fun, suggests a degree of danger both real and imagined. When things gets scary, Mommy gets blamed—but since it's difficult to hate Mommy outright, she might create a scary monster in the closet or a wolf at the door. In the traditional version, making the wrong choices out in the world leads to disaster. The wolf blows down the houses and then eats the first two piglets. Only the most painstaking piglet succeeds in defeating the wolf. In kinder versions, bad choices lead to second chances. Together, in the solid brick house of the third piglet, the pig brothers turn the wolf into stew and live happily ever after.

Mrs. Pig's parenting skills were pretty good: she taught her sons to be self-reliant individuals and to support each other. That's a great story to hear repeatedly, for both mother and the children. The pigs, like children, are little but capable; innocent and creative; they conquer their fears and actual threats.

IRRESISTIBLE AUTHORS PAUL GALDONE

Three Little Kittens, The Three Bears, The Little Red Hen: these timeless tales are retold and drawn so persuasively by masterful artist Paul Galdone that they invite enjoyable hours of rereading and looking. Once you and your child have gone through them a few times, you will be able to close your eyes and still see and hear the teeny-tiny woman and the three little bears, goats, kittens, and pigs. Galdone's illustrations are easily understood and enlivened with particular details for children looking closely. The wolf in *The Three Little Pigs* has eyes that focus on the pig quite intensely, and their communication is clear. Three different fonts highlight the big, middle, and little wee bears' bowls and chairs. Galdone's pictures never become dated.

Cultural Dimensions to Fairy Tales

All fairy tales deal with conflict. Historically, fairy tales have been women's stories, and were told rather than written. Perhaps that's why so many of the stories concern girls successfully overcoming distressing situations, and often via magical means. The Brothers Grimm collected their tales from peasants; the French writer Perrault collected, embellished, and composed stories to amuse the king and his court. Hans Christian Andersen wrote his own.

Because these stories are so deeply entrenched in Western culture, the most casual reference to them can serve to make a point. Modern authors seem to love to use them as jumping off points, creating new versions or picking up where the old story left off. You can do the same, if you want to keep the story going.

But What about the Scary Ones?

It's happened to all of us. You turn the page, and there it is—a scary monster, a burning house, a whipping—something you're just not sure how to handle. Maybe it's the giant in *Jack and the Beanstalk* about to devour the boy. Maybe it's a character trapped in front of an oncoming train. Do you boldly read on or do a panicked, on-the-spot revision? Take a deep breath and read on. It's just a book—and that's just the point. Many parents worry that by reading about scary things, they're introducing them to their child. But the fears are already there. Have you ever thought about how many "giants" there are in a baby's life? Or how a looming face appears to your baby? What if the face says, "I'd love to eat you all up!"?

Got monsters? Try helping your child play with the monsters in different ways. Have him help you draw a monster. He can add the hair or choose the colors. He could pretend to be a monster, with or without a hand-created brown-bag monster mask. Make the whole thing extra silly, fun, and playful—and make the point, again and again, that monsters are just pretend.

Fears—of the dark, of imaginary monsters, of dogs or puppets or clowns—are natural and ingrained. We pretty much all start with some of them. Seeing the fear represented in a book validates the fear and puts it into context. Other people are scared. Other people come out okay. It's okay to be scared. Fairy tales and other stories put voice to our fears and allow us to conquer them. You may think it's never occurred to your child that you (or she) could die. You're probably wrong. Making death, or any other fear, into an unmentionable only makes it more frightening. A matter-of-fact reading of a fairy tale—death, teeth, and monsters intact—simplified for the youngest listeners, yet safely removed from reality, lets those fears out in the open and gives them an airing. Fairy tales encourage children to use their imagination to overcome their fears.

Cinderella and the Magic Culture Mirror

The Cinderella story is ubiquitous. Its handling of extended family situations may not be entirely politically correct, but all the same, it speaks to us. We all want Daddy's love and the Prince—boys too.

Where it originated is unknown, but the earliest datable version of the Cinderella story occurs in a Chinese book written about 850–860 AD. The earliest European version of the tale was published in Italy in 1634. In 1697 Perrault introduced the story familiar to most Americans, *Cinderella*, or *The Tale of the Little Glass Slipper* in his *Histories or Tales of Past Times*. Some of the earliest versions have a talking tree and plenty of blood. More than seven hundred variations of the tale have been collected from around the world over the centuries, and it appears in almost every language. Amazon.com lists over one thousand Cinderella titles, from Appalachia and Africa to China and Korea to the Middle East and Turkey.

Such a universal story must have a universal appeal. At its core, it's a story of a girl abandoned/orphaned by her mother's death and her father's remarriage. She's displaced, angry, and alone. But she dreams of a magic rescue, and what's even better, she gets it, while those around her get theirs. Her situation speaks to our deepest fears; her triumph delights us.

Contemporary versions for all ages abound, from *Pretty Woman* to *Harry Potter* to the Disney cartoon. Everything and everyone—sports teams, businesses, and nations—can be a "Cinderella story." It's a metaphor for the indomitable human spirit.

Fairy Tale Collections to Make You Happy Ever After

It's rare to find a fairy tale collection truly targeted at babies, toddlers, and twos. Here are a few of the simplest with plenty of pictures. You may find yourself needing to abridge the text a bit for some toddlers and two-year-olds; others will be ready to enjoy them in full. Either way, since you'll be reading from these for years, they're a good investment.

- **Fairy Tale Classic: Easy-to-Read Collection,** Harriet Ziefert, Emily Bolam (illus.). Includes retellings of *The Gingerbread Boy, The Little Red Hen, Little Red Riding Hood,* and *The Ugly Duckling.* This collection has Ziefert's golden touch; like all her books, it's clear, accessible, and age appropriate.

- **Golden Books Treasury of Elves and Fairies,** Jane Werner Watson, Garth Williams (illus.). Another beloved treasury reprinted to the joy of all. The illustrations form a basis for what some of us think these little creatures (like the Little Mermaid) actually look like. Squint your eyes and you'll see them again too.

- **The Helen Oxenbury Nursery Collection,** Helen Oxenbury. Ms. Oxenbury's rendering of popular verses, rhymes, and tales are always perfect for our babies.

- **The Tall Book of Nursery Tales,** Aleksey Ivanov (illus.). Promises to be an easily accessible, well-drawn collection of old favorites.

- **The Golden Book of Fairy Tales,** Adrienne Segur (illus.). This "Once upon a time" collection is a beloved favorite by many parents and grandparents because of the illustrations and renderings. It might be too advanced in words and with pictures imprecisely paired with text for our age group but an oversized and much valued contribution to anyone's library.

- **Nursery Classics,** Paul Galdone. Beautiful illustrations with plenty of detail fill this collection of four classic but simple tales.

Out There without a Net:
Making Up Your Own Stories

From getting comfortable telling stories aloud from a book, it's just a short step to soloing—that is, telling stories without the book. "Tell me a story" is a classic child's plea to stave off bedtime, pass waiting time, or just because it seems like a good time for a snuggle. So there you sit, child in your arms and you begin: Once upon a time…

Once upon a time what? Suddenly this is harder than it sounded. A prince? A princess?

You don't know anything about princes and princesses. You don't want this just to be some rehash of something you read, do you? Wait, that's not a bad idea. If there are only seven plots in the world, there's no sense coming up with a new story.

So maybe you tell a story you already know, a truncated version of the *Three Little Pigs* or the book you read last night with an owl for a hero instead of a rabbit. That's fair. Or maybe a story about your child would be best. You relate the events of the day, ending each with and then…and then… You might even send your child off in a rocket to the moon, only to discover that you have disappointingly little for her to do once she gets there.

There's something about "Once upon a time" that can be intimidating. It sets the bar too high. Start with something different, like "once there was a little boy who..." or "I once knew a dog who..." The story might flow a little more easily.

Afterwards, she seems satisfied, but you may be feeling a bit inept. Haven't you read interviews with authors who say their books came directly from the stories they told their own children? Yours didn't sound like a book. It sounded, well, a bit bald. No dialogue. Not much adventure. Why bother?

Why Tell Stories?

When you tell a story rather than reading one, your child has to listen without any aids to focus her attention. She has to imagine the scenes, the people, the colors, all for herself and remember what's going on without the help of a picture.

When you tell a story, whether it's a personal one or your rendition of a fairy tale, you tailor your words to your baby. Focus on what she knows, where she's been, and what interests her. You can tell her about the three little pigs' mother, or what kind of shoes they like to wear. You can tell her about something you did when you were little that's just like something she did today. She's your baby, and you know what she likes better than anyone else.

Telling stories about your childhood, or even about your day, deepens your connection to one another. Telling fantastical stories about her helps her to dream, to see herself in ways she'd never imagined, and to begin to imagine them. Even putting your own spin on a book she's heard many times is a great way to reinforce her natural creativity (who says the sky has to be blue every time?).

Telling the Stories You Know

Some stories you tell naturally. You may not feel your toddler is ready for the one about the fraternity guy you knew who mooned the president of the college, but you probably have a few of those honed and ready for dinner with friends. You can tell stories about her day in the same way. It doesn't matter that she was there, she'll still enjoy it, especially if you build up to what was, to her, the high point. A story that starts with breakfast, crescendos at a garbage truck emptying a dumpster, and then ends with arrival at daycare might not thrill your buddies, but this audience will appreciate it. A young baby will enjoy a gentle, even droning narration of her day as she falls asleep. No need to reach a high point for her.

Stories about your childhood will also come naturally. "When I was your age," they begin, and go on from there. Toddlers love simple stories about how Grandma made Mommy pancakes every Saturday or soup when she was sick. You may even find he has an unusual fascination with some character and wants to hear more about your childhood dog or even the funny guy at work who dropped a box of files down the stairs. Those requests could be your jumping off point into fiction. You have an established character who's already captured his attention, now you only need to make up a story to go along with it.

> *"I told my daughter a story every night when I got home from work, starting when she was very small. By the time she was three, it was a real ritual for us, and the stories started getting really complicated. I couldn't just wing it—I'd make up something to happen in the car on the way home from work. It's actually really fun for me, too. She's six now, and currently in a hot air balloon with a monkey and a toaster on her way to Peru (sometimes she helps with the plotting)."* —Jim

CAPER: Making It Up as You Go

At some point in the first three years of raising your child, you're going to find yourself making up a story from scratch. Maybe you've always imagined a child who'd say, "Tell me a story," maybe you're continuing a tradition you loved as a kid, or maybe you're just stuck in traffic, or a waiting room, or at the airport. Most kids love these homemade tales. Maybe it's just the sheer joy of having something they know you're creating just for them.

Making up a story on the fly is harder than it sounds. You're going to need characters, action, a bit of dialogue, and, if you're up to it, a problem and a resolution. We've even come up with a formula: CAPeR. Characters, Action, Problem, Resolution. So: Big and Little find a ball. "I want it," says one. "No, I want it," says the other. They pull and pull on the ball until it bursts. They cry. "I have some tape," says Big. "I'll hold the pieces together," says Little. So they tape it together, Big blows it up, and they decide to play catch. The end.

Not destined for a starred review in *Library Journal* but enough, with some embellishment, to entertain a baby or toddler in line at the grocery store. If you've got a gift for storytelling, you're golden. If not, maybe CAPeR will help. Either way, you're guaranteed to please your audience—and by the time he's old enough to want a little more action, you can encourage your child to chime in.

Ages and Stages:
Story Telling and Fairy Tales

Newborn	• Read everything aloud, from the instructions on the back of the instant coffee to junk mail. If you're looking at the words, share! • Bedtime stories always start the same way (Once upon a time; Once there was a little girl named…) and end the same way (And then they all slept all night through). It doesn't matter what you put in between.
Heads Up	• Be prepared to get down on the floor with your tiny one and have a conversation eye to eye. It's such an effort to raise your head but having Mommy or Daddy's smiling face greet you makes it worthwhile.
Sitting	• Find some clever oven gloves to use for puppet-like stories. • Act out a silly simple story between two toys. They could play hide and seek, or just jump up and down and talk to each other.
Crawling/Creeping	• Do read the same books over and over. At this stage, she's just beginning to make a connection between what you say and the pictures. • If you're condensing a fairy tale, try to keep in the key phrases (Once upon a time, And he huffed and he puffed and he BLEW the house down) so that they'll stay consistent as you read more of the story.

Cruising/Walking	• Tell a bedtime story about their day and all of their wonderful accomplishments. • Chose a few books with a consistent character and try giving that character a special voice.
Talking (a few words)	• Ask your child for one or two or three things to put in the story: a girl, a dog, and a ball. Then tell that story!
Talking More	• She can start learning the names of a few favorite books. Make sure you're reading both the title and author, too, so she can start learning how to ask for it. • Open up a new wordless book and ask her what she can name that she sees.
Running (but not talking much)	• Act out fairy tales with lots of action, like *The Gingerbread Boy* and *The Three Little Pigs*. • Look for books that encourage you to interact, to tickle and grab one another as you read aloud, like *Pete's a Pizza*.
Talking ALL THE TIME!	• Get the children to help you read the story by leaving off the last word, or by asking what happens next. • Make "mistakes" in reading on purpose. See what happens. • Compare and contrast version of favorite fairy tales.

Chapter Five:
Judge a Book by Its Cover:
Art in Your Life

Telling a story through pictures is an ancient tradition for human beings. All art and literature began with early efforts at communication: in French and Spanish cave paintings; Egyptian mummies and tombs; and Eskimo ivory carvings. These were outlined images or silhouettes of animals, finger drawings on clay, and imprints of hands. Abstract symbols emerged. Written communication came much later, and began with stylized symbols called hieroglyphs. Further refinement developed as pictographs—pictures representing what was being described or tallied. Those pictographs gradually began to represent concepts and ideas and finally, sounds. Even today, when we want to be absolutely sure our meaning is understood, we often turn to art. "Let me draw you a picture. "

What Can Babies See?

Object and face recognition: At birth, babies can see your face from arm's length, but they seem to prefer borders and often gaze at the hairline. By two months they hone in on your features (like nose and mouth) and by three to five months (if not earlier) can distinguish mom's face from a stranger's.

Focusing: Infants start life far-sighted. By two to three months most infants focus accurately.

Eye-Coordination and Tracking: Newborns can track an object if it's large enough, has good contrast, and moves slowly. By three months this ability is well established.

Color: By two to six weeks, infants can distinguish a red from a green object. Detecting pastels and other subtle colors will take time to develop.

Pictures Are Worth a Thousand Words

The pictures in children's books absolutely qualify as art. They tell stories, convey emotion, capture attention, and bring pleasure. Where else can you find art that is universally approachable, speaking to young and old and in between? A picture book is itself an art form that fits in your hands.

For babies, toddlers, and twos, picture books are the only books, and in a very real sense, the artwork is the book. For now, she's concentrating on visual literacy. The words are just squiggles—part of the art. But "reading" the artwork now leads to reading words later. Your baby's bookshelves are already filled with art. Some of it is elaborate and exceptional, some not-so-great but still much loved and full of communication. Understanding how the artists arrange elements like color, line, shape, and movement to tell the story can make reading with your baby that much more fun.

Baby's First Art

- **I Kissed the Baby!,** Mary Elizabeth Murphy. Brightly colored animals against a black background welcome the baby duck with tickling, singing, and a kiss from Mama.

- **A Magical Day with Matisse,** Julie Merberg. Lilting, rhyming text invites the reader into ten Matisse paintings.

- **Winter Friends,** Carl R. Sams II and Jean Stoick. Big photos of winter scenes, with small sparks of color, will entrance all ages.

- **A Color of His Own,** Leo Lionni. A chameleon is blue because he can't find a color of his own, until he finds a friend to share his constantly changing shade.

- **Baby Pets,** Margaret Miller. Adorable photographs of real babies and real pets will please everyone.

- **Out to Play,** Michel Blake. Each page of this easy-to-open board book features a brightly colored object for a black and white photographed preschooler to play with. (Also *Off to Bed*.)

Artists and art editors consider each detail:

- Size
- Shape
- End papers and loose covers in hardcover editions
- Title placement, fonts, and style
- Text color, font, size, placement on the page
- Borders
- Bar codes

The dust jacket of any hardcover you buy can make great art for a baby or toddler's room, especially hung in a group with a theme, like trains or a specific illustrator. Any framing place can dry mount them to prevent wrinkling, or you can trim them yourself and slide them into inexpensive frames with pre-cut mats. Hardcover books may be expensive, but at least you get a bonus gift!

Visual Literacy: Learning to Read the World

So why does this matter? Aren't the pictures just there to give the baby something to look at while you read? Why make such a big deal about "art"?

Visual literacy is important because we live in an increasingly visual culture filled with images that communicate a surprising amount of information. By looking at and talking about what we see, we help our children to understand even more of the world, long before they have words of their own to describe what they see and understand.

{ *David's brother gave him a favorite book to read to his six-month-old nephew. "Show him one page at a time," the brother cautioned, "because he goes nuts when you show him a two-page spread." David dutifully began reading the board book of shapes to the baby, and then was overcome with curiosity. When he presented the baby with two pages at once, the little guy began to get agitated and make pre-crying noises. Quickly David turned the page and held one page in front of the baby. Disaster averted; happiness restored.* }

Both infants and young children experience the world through their senses rather than words. It's your comforting tone, not the words of your lullaby, that soothes him to sleep. When it comes to reading, the words are only beginning to be more than pleasurable sounds. But the pictures, the pictures are everything. Most babies are taking in much of their new world through their eyes, and it all goes by fast. Pictures in books hold still and provide a chance to examine the world and all its many elements in a handy portable format.

The art in books does three things for your baby. First, it holds still and focuses his attention. He can look at a picture of a bowl of cereal without being distracted by a kitchen full of movement and objects, and he can enjoy it visually without anyone trying to feed it to him. Second, he gets to read. Someone has depicted a bowl of cereal and he's interpreting that picture. He can have time to think about cereal, or notice that the bowl has a small puppy decoration on it. He can even touch the page and move his hand to his mouth, indicating a complete comprehension of cereal as something that one eats. Third, pictures (just like words) can mean more than they say. He learns to read the emotions in the pictures. He sees that the baby in the picture is angrily pushing the cereal bowl away, or eating happily, and he gets a sense of what is happening.

Find out what art excites your baby. If he's mobile or can sit up and grab, line up two or three strikingly different books at the same distance from him. Which one does he go for first: The colorful or the black-and-white? Busy or simple? (This is going to work best at home, rather than in a new and distracting environment like the library or a bookstore.)

At the core of all visual literacy lies the ability to understand and enjoy pictures and all they communicate—and for that, your baby may be better equipped than you are! If there's one thing a baby can do, it's look. After all, that's how babies spend their time—sleeping, eating, and looking. With their eyes, and later with their hands, they're discovering what's near and what's far, where edges are, which objects have dimension and which are pictures or patterns on a page. They're not merely looking, they're learning to visually interpret the world.

TALKING TO THE ARTIST PAT CUMMINGS

"In books, it's unfair to mislead readers by showing expressions that don't convey the mood/message. In *Ananse*, the lizard HAS to have a glint in his eye even while smiling. I ask the really little kids if Ananse should trust him and they shake their heads vigorously because they already know the smile is too sly. No poker faces allowed in picture books. Even if it's merely a raised eyebrow or a crooked smile, something's gotta give a clue to the emotions."

Behind the Scenes:
The Elements of Children's Book Art

Trust us. Understanding a few basic elements of art will enrich the experience of reading with your child and help you enjoy watching her entering the world of visual communication. You'll see how much the artists' choice of elements such as style, color, and point of view help your baby to read and understand the story better. These are the specifics of visual literacy and they appear whether the artist works in watercolor, collages, cartoons, photographs, drawings, or constructed interactive pop-ups/lift-the-flaps.

Encourage your child to pick a favorite color among the many in a really colorful book, and don't press her to make the same choice every time. Why did she choose that color today? How do you know it's her favorite and not your choice for her?

Artists use line, color, shape, and space as tools to create works of art. These elements operate in every piece of artwork, including your child's scribbles. With the exception of color, it's difficult to isolate these elements—lines create shapes that define space. But it's the principles created by the combined elements—balance, spatial relations, emphasis, and patterns—that your baby is absorbing with every picture she examines. Every book she looks at, from picture books to cloth books to books shaped like dinosaurs, will establish and reinforce these basic principles.

Visual Elements and Principles

- **Color:** All colors are mixed from three primaries: red, blue, and yellow, shaded by the addition of black or tinted by adding white.
- **Line:** A line is the track made by a point moving in space.
- **Shape:** Wherever the ends of a continuous line meet, a shape is formed.
- **Space:** Space can be two-dimensional, three-dimensional, negative (as in background space, or the space between the legs of a chair) or positive (the chair itself).
- **Balance:** The arrangement of the lines, shapes, and colors on the page creates (or intentionally avoids) a balanced scene.
- **Emphasis/Spatial Relationships:** The eye of the viewer will focus first on an area of emphasis or center of interest. Includes perspective, proportions, and positional placing of objects in picture
- **Pattern/Rhythm:** Repeated shapes, lines, or colors create movement and rhythm in a composition.

Color

Color is both the most obvious and the most commonly discussed element of visual literacy. Every parent likes to name colors and teach them to their babies. Color saturates most board books and picture books. Bright color focuses the eye and mind. Babies, toddlers, and two-year-olds all respond to colors and enjoy making some personal interpretation about them. For example, Molly Bang's eponymous ball in *Yellow Ball* stands out on every page as it travels from one family's beach game out to sea and into the arms of a new welcoming child. The color helps convey an emotion: we root for the bright ball in the actively whirling dark and scary ocean storm. In making her ball yellow, Ms. Bang communicates something wholesome and hopeful. The ball is a glowing orb and a comforting companion. Yellow is a color of happy contentment. A violet ball would make a very different story.

Avoid "washable" crayons. Regular crayons rarely mark on clothes and scrape off most surfaces—but for some reason, the washable red one stains like nothing else!

Dark colors in books for very young children are much less common. Books like *Owl Babies,* in blacks, grays, and blues, stand out on the shelves and in the readers' minds. The blues and blacks of the night surround the artist Patrick Benson's white baby owls, and heighten a feeling of anxiety they experience over their mother's absence. These "dark" books aren't necessarily somber or ominous, but the use of darker colors does effectively enhance the mood of the story and contrasts strongly with most other books for kids.

Books about colors are common, which only makes the uncommonly good ones stand out all the more.

- **Why Is Blue Dog Blue?,** George Rodrigue. "Artists don't have to paint things the way they really are."

- **Mouse Paint,** Ellen Stoll Walsh. Three white mice hop, mix, and splash dance in their color puddles, mixing new colors as they move.

- **Color Dance,** Ann Jonas. Four young children in colored leotards dance with joyous abandon, using colored scarves to demonstrate how colors mix.

- **Is It Red? Is It Yellow? Is It Blue?,** Tana Hoban. Vibrant and real photographs capture everyday colorful things seen in the city.

- **Cat's Colors,** Jane Cabrera. This is a cat's colorful search for its favorite color, with enough story to help grown-up readers go through color choices cheerfully.

- **Color Farm,** Lois Ehlert. This board book employs shapes and cutouts in bright colors to create the animals, all with the same bright green eye (created by a cutout to the back page of the book).

- **Frederick,** Leo Lionni. While most of the mice scurry about collecting food for the approaching winter, Frederick gathers intangibles like sunrays, colors, and words. His word pictures nourish the downcast mice with warmth and imagination during the dark season.

- **The Black and White Book: El Libro Blanco y Negro,** Alejandra Longo, Daniel Chaskielberg (illus.). Bright and basic objects in white and black. (Also *The Red Book: El Libro Rojo, The Green Book: El Libro Verde.*)

Line

A line is where a drawing starts. Lines, beginning with one dot, lead our eyes and define the shape. The lines can be thick or thin, curved, broken, or wavy, and appear in any color. They can outline a form or create a landscape or a nose in a single stroke.

Line is the foundation of everything: art, design, and alphabet. A child's first drawings are all lines: round scribbles, dark zigzags up and down the page. Later the lines become things, and later still they form letters, words, and full-blown illustrated manuscripts.

What is the impact of line on the readers? We know that line directs our attention and defines the image. But the quality of the line also affects our feelings about the images and pictures. Some lines make us feel the solidity of an object or activity of the person. A character's body sitting stiffly erect, with thick straight balanced lines, conveys one thing; curvy and lightly drawn lines convey another. Angled eyebrow lines show surprise or happiness or anger or fear. Is the character seemingly drawn with a few lines, in a fluid don't-take-the-pencil-off-the-paper way; or are there lots of scratches that might create a feeling of hyperactivity? Line, like color, can carry emotional weight.

Featured Book

Harold and the Purple Crayon

Crockett Johnson

In this delightful book by author/illustrator Crockett Johnson, line is everything. Harold draws a thick purple line that becomes each landscape—a tree, the ocean, the city. This line has held the attention of generations of children as Harold draws—and lives—anything he can imagine. Maybe Harold reminds us all that simple creativity can add a lot to life. If you can draw a moon, you need never walk without moonlight.

Shape

Shapes help us organize our world. Wherever the ends of a continuous line meet, a shape is formed. Shapes come, well, in all shapes: circular, oval, square, triangular, and amorphic, which is a non-geometric free-form. Geometric shapes such as circles, triangles, or squares have perfect, uniform measurements and don't often appear in nature. Organic shapes are associated with things from the natural world, like plants and animals.

One fun feature of shapes is that they can become tangible. You can do more than just put them on paper. You can cut them out, hold them in your hand, and share them. Shapes put boundaries on things. It's a way of organizing our world, and recognizing things that are similar and those that are different.

Shapely Favorites

- **Little Cloud,** Eric Carle. Clouds transform into a plane, a shark, and a clown, and then back into a cloud among clouds.

- **My Shapes/Mis Formas,** Rebecca Emberley. Shapes are bilingual and bold for toddlers.

- **Changes, Changes,** Pat Hutchins. This thirty-five-year-old favorite wordless book tells a tale of family hardships and affection by shifting shapes into houses and fire engines.

- **Shapes, Shapes, Shapes,** Tana Hoban. Real objects are photographed as the round, square, and triangular—and fun—objects they are.

- **Round Is a Mooncake: A Book of Shapes,** Roseanne Thong, Grace Lin (illus.). This concept book brings in a new Asian sensibility for shaped items, and begs us to begin to look around to find circles, triangles, and squares of our own.

- **Shapes (Slide 'n' Seek),** Chuck Murphy. Hidden pictures reveal real things that are also shapes.

Why else do we enjoy teaching our children about shapes? Like color, geometric shapes offer something clear to learn, and there are lots of books to help teach them. It's even more fun to spot the shapes in the books you already have: the round wheel, the rectangular windows.

Books themselves often are shaped or small. Think of those board books of snowmen or puppies. These are generally small enough to be held easily by a baby or toddler. Beatrix Potter designed small books for small hands about one hundred years ago. The shape was classic, the size was not, and it changed the world of books forevermore.

Space, Balance, and Perspective

For the most part, we all find pleasure in balance. Symmetry is our default setting, and we gain a measure of assured comfort when things conform to our expectations. Babies quickly begin to recognize balance or the lack of it. They'll spot a table with only three and a half legs or a fishbowl balancing on an umbrella and recognize the problem long before they can put words to it.

But asymmetry can be remarkably effective. A slide is a slide, and fun, partly because it's a line on a diagonal, or spiral. A swing at rest is a stable, squared-off shape, but becomes thrilling when moving in an arc. Drawings use balance—or its absence—

Featured Book

How Do Dinosaurs Say Good Night?

Jane Yolen, Mark Teague (illus.)

When ordinary suburban human parents try to tuck their enormous darlings into bed, they need LOTS of room. The artist uses skewed and dramatic perspectives to incorporate the huge dinosaurs who soar up to their ceilings, dwarf their beds, and tower over their shrimpy parents.

to engage our emotions so we feel that the character is safe or in danger depending on the pitch of the line.

Think of an empty room. Where do you place the things to maximize the space? Do you pile all the stuff into one corner of the room, or balance things out pleasingly, and artfully? The same problem confronts every artist who starts with a blank page.

In general, artists help the baby readers to focus on the one or two important visuals as they read through the book by using and defining space—leaving the background blank, for example, or filling it with a familiar or unfamiliar scene. In her *Max and Ruby* board books, Rosemary Wells focuses on the characters and important props. The background is just a colored page—negative space that isn't Max, or a bathtub. In her picture books for older toddlers and preschoolers, Ms. Wells elaborates Ruby and Max's background with patterned wallpaper, sofas, and kitchen cabinets—and takes up the whole page.

Dr. Seuss focuses on the characters without much identifying background information, and, in doing so, he skews both balance and perspective. We get the feeling of slight anarchy, even in the simplest *Hop on Pop*. Most of Seussean background is white with the characters not needing any particular location. If location is key, it's sized and shaped to suit the scene. A huge train can balance on a tiny, precarious track without concerning the characters at all—although it may concern some readers! One librarian said she hated the work of Dr. Seuss when she was a child. She liked knowing what things really were. She liked order. Dr. Seuss's worlds seemed chaotic and messy. Anything could and did happen, and she was unable to enjoy his wit. It took years before she understood how other children adored his slip-slapping, pop-hopping, witty art and rhyme.

> "At two and a half, Sam is fascinated by airplanes: real ones, toy ones, books, pictures. As he talks about them, it's clear he's struggling to grasp perspective. He points to the picture of the plane about to take off and exclaims, 'It's too big to fly!' On the next page, as the plane recedes into the distant clouds, he tells me, 'See, it has to get little to go up up up in the air!' Later, as a passenger in a real plane, he tells me that we are 'getting littler' as we take off. I explain, but I don't think I changed his mind." —KJ

Artists employ tricks to make things appear to be smaller (or less important) the farther away they are from us. The artist reveals her point of view by placing the objects in the picture frame. One look at Vera B. Williams's lucky babies in *"More More More," Said the Baby* proves the point. Those babies are clearly VIP STARS, and it's not hard to guess Ms. Williams' point of view about the centrality of babies.

Have your toddler or older child write and illustrate a book to be read to a new baby. She can dictate the words of the story to you (and even get your help with some drawings) or just read it from her own pictures. No matter where the book stands on the "art" spectrum, baby will be thrilled by so much attention from a big sib.

Perspective also tells us many things about the relationship of the characters. Who's up close, and what's farther away? Which one is the king or the important character? The artist's perspective can shift us into unexpected places, as in Jon Muth's retelling of *Stone Soup*, where the reader sees all the villagers peering down at her from around the rim of the soup pot. Grasping the picture is a real leap for a child, who may at first be mystified by the perspective from inside the pot.

Pattern, Rhythm, and Movement

You probably think of rhythm in connection with poems and songs, but what about in art? Pictures have rhythm, and movement, too. The artist creates movement by repeating shapes, lines, or colors. An undulating line suggests movement and flow, like a wave on the shore. Curves and arcs suggest movement, too. As a whole, each picture moves you through the story, through the setting, or through time.

> *"My two-year-old Dylan keeps making me turn the page before I'm finished with the words. He's just finished with that picture. It's like he's reading to a different rhythm. I do my best to work with him and follow the story so that we can still enjoy reading together."* —Denise

Patterns are repeated in alternating rhythms of color, texture, shape, or images. "Cumulative" books, which repeat the same pattern of animals and dialogue on each page with a slight variation, are great examples of pattern that appears in both words and pictures. ("There Was an Old Woman Who Swallowed a Fly" would be a cumulative song.) The predictable pattern is both comforting and empowering—the youngest reader can figure out what to expect.

Cumulative Books That Take Us Along for the Ride

- **When the Elephant Walks,** Keiko Kasza. This cumulative story reveals we're all afraid of something. The bear scares the crocodile, and the crocodile scares the wild hog and so it goes.

- **Mr. Gumpy's Motor Car,** John Burningham. The children and various animals pile into the car with the kindly Mr. Gumpy, and although, as we say when each animal gets in, it's a squash, all goes well until it starts to rain, and every animal has a reason not to get out and push.

- **The Napping House,** Audrey Wood, Don Wood (illus.). More and more children and pets move steadily forward to share Granny's bed.

- **Oh, Look!,** Patricia Polacco. When three goats escape their pen and head for the fair, every page brings a new obstacle to overcome in this clever take on the Going on a Bear Hunt rhyme.

- **Duck in the Truck,** Jez Alborough. A rollicking rhyming book about the duck in his truck getting stuck in the muck, and helped by three animal friends.

- **The Doorbell Rang,** Pat Hutchins. The doorbell rings and brings more and more friends to share delicious cookies.

The Art of...Enjoying the Art

Art is enriching, constant, and comforting. While every picture contains certain familiar elements, looking at each new image offers an opportunity for endless imaginings. Taking in whatever is there to see is the baby's whole experience at that moment, her immediate reality. She studies every element on the page, both entering into and taking things out of the artist's world. Adults are quick to turn the page or get the babies to help to do it. Slow down! She's still looking, drinking in the sights and absorbing the information. Although we can't be sure what she thinks of the picture, we have evidence that she's responding. How do we know? Does your child return to a particular picture time and again? Does she smile? Does she lean in to go nose to nose with the character, stroke the pet, or even mimic the character's face? Or wave her arms in excitement when shown a picture of a cow?

TALKING TO THE ARTIST   LOIS EHLERT

My mother used to read the same book to all three of us kids. So in the books I create, I try to extend the age levels up and down so that every reader gets something. A beginning reader, for instance, might just read the large text, and an advanced reader might read the subtext or little labels which have more complicated words. I try to make sure they don't get bored. The really little ones can read the pictures.

I also love music; I love the sounds of the human voice. Although I started out being an artist, I am always conscious of how the words sound, and the rhythm of the sentence structure. I make sure that I lay out the design so it does not break the line for the person reading aloud.

For example, *Feathers for Lunch* features a woodpecker. Not only are some words and labels written in red but so are the sounds important to the story, like the *jingle jingle* of the cat's bell. In one place the woodpecker is pecking on the tree looking for ants, and I have four or five ants walking up the dark bark offering little surprises to test children's visual literacy.

Children don't always want to reread a book. If they only read it once, there's something not quite right.

My Aunt Came Back

Pat Cummings

This book's cover artwork radiates color and life, signaling something important and setting the whole book in motion. A grown woman and a young girl are linked by hands and eyes, dancing together between a bright blue sky with puffy clouds above and some wavy waves of the sea below. Their clothes are bright; their hair and body language is full of movement. Immediately, you know this is going to be a lively read.

The lilting, rhythmic story is heavily accented poetry like a song: My aunt came back from Timbuktu. She brought me back a wooden shoe. The words literally dance up and down across the page to keep the rhythm going. In the background a small dwelling in Timbuktu is connected to an apartment building in New York by the curve of the earth. The traveling aunt lifts her equally excited niece high off the ground in a joyous reunion. We are given details of Timbuktu's housing, and a typical wooden shoe gift, so different from a New York apartment building and sneakers.

Pat Cummings's brown-skinned figures are outlined and stylized, somewhere between cartoonesque and realistic, and animated with curves, smiles, gifts, and colors that create a vibrancy. Wouldn't each one of us love to have an aunt like this? And a joyous niece? The exuberant affection between the aunt and niece pours forth: in their gestures and touching connection, the vivid colors, and the rhythm of both words and pictures.

For you, a new appreciation of art can make reading together more fun. You'll begin to recognize certain artists. KJ's husband spotted Ian Falconer's style (*Olivia*) immediately on a cover of *The New Yorker*. You may even pick up some technique. Soon enough, your child is going to be begging you to draw pictures for her. It's nice if you can create a recognizable dog. At the very least, trying to figure out what makes Helen Oxenbury's round baby faces with dot eyes and line smiles so much more charming than yours might occupy you during your fourteenth reading of *Goodnight, Baby*.

Great Books for Making Art with Your Baby and Toddler

- ***10 Minute Activities: Fun Things to Do for You and Your Child,*** Manufactured by Priddy Bicknell, Andrea Pinnington

- ***Ed Emberley's Drawing Book of Animals,*** Ed Emberley

- ***Young at Art: Teaching Toddlers Self-Expression, Problem-Solving Skills, and an Appreciation of Art,*** Susan Striker

- ***My Art Class and My Animal Art Class,*** Nellie Shepherd

- ***Wonderplay: Interactive and Developmental Games, Crafts, and Creative Activities for Infants, Toddlers, and Preschoolers,*** Fretta Reitzes, Beth Teitelman, Lois A. Mark

Great Books about Kids Making Art

- **The Dot,** Peter H. Reynolds. "I can't do it" becomes "I'm an artist" when a simple dot, treated like a masterpiece, inspires more.

- **I Ain't Gonna Paint No More!,** Karen Beaumont, David Catrow (illus.). When her son paints every bit of the house, Mama declares that he ain't gonna paint no more...but with wild colorful splatters and the gradual obliteration of any white space on the page, he proves her wrong on a new canvas, painting every body part.

- **A Brave Spaceboy: Moving Is an Adventure!,** Dana Kessimakis Smith, Laura Freeman (illus.). Kids moving into a new home create outer space vehicles with the empty boxes.

- **Setting the Turkeys Free,** W. Nikola-Lisa, Ken Wilson-Max (illus.). When hand-print collage turkeys look so real that a fox goes after them, their creator sets them free—then lures them back again. Every toddler and preschooler will recognize a familiar art project.

- **Emma's Rug,** Allen Say. This story of a child whose mother inadvertently alters her most-loved possession (and, Emma believes, the source of her art) by washing it may speak more to older children, but the need to trust your own creative spirit applies at any age. A powerfully beautiful book.

- **Pete's Chicken,** Harriet Ziefert, Laura Rader (illus.). Preschool artist Pete's chicken doesn't look like anyone else's. He's remarkably resilient and therefore triumphant.

Beautiful Books for Sharing
Showcasing the Elements

These are books that focus on one or more of the individual elements of art: shape and color, line and balance. They tend to be on the simpler side, but should remain relevant as your baby grows into a toddler and beyond.

- ***At the Firehouse,*** Anne Rockwell. Wonderful for its colors and the absence of outlines on the characters and scenes—objects are delineated only by the change in color.

- ***Barnyard Banter,*** Denise Fleming. Fleming's unique pulp painting medium holds the reader on every page. It's one of the best noisy animal books ever, with a remarkable textural quality.

- ***Ben's Trumpet,*** Rachel Isadora. Brilliant use of line. The young boy and all the language surrounding him perfectly reflect the zigzag rhythm of this jazzy story in black and white.

- ***The Day the Babies Crawled Away,*** Peggy Rathmann. A preschooler chases the escaping babies at a picnic with the illustrations presented almost entirely in silhouette. Cool and fascinating.

- ***It Looked Like Spilt Milk,*** Charles G. Shaw. Bold white clouds on bright blue sky suggest shapes of known and inventive creatures.

- ***Noah's Ark,*** Lucy Cousins. Cousins (of Maisy fame) offers her trademark childlike drawings, bright colors, and patterns to spark up a familiar story.

- ***Owen's Marshmallow Chick,*** Kevin Henkes. Owen, a delightful line-drawing of a mouse, gets an equally delightful and colorful Easter basket and makes a friend out of the candy chick.

- ***1, 2, 3, Follow Me,*** Phillipe Dupasquier. The pages are shaped like numbers, and on each, increasing numbers of cumulative animals chase each other until ten delivers a big surprise.

- **Look-Alikes Jr.,** Joan Steiner. This artist uses small found objects from various rooms in the house to create the rooms in miniature, prompting you and your child to spot a bed built with crayons and pasta and other tiny eye-teasers.

- **Rosie's Walk,** Pat Hutchins. Hutchins's famous hen outsmarts a fox in perfectly complementary designs and colors. Broad, almost physical humor for all.

- **Swimmy,** Leo Lionni. One black fish in a sea of red fish beckons readers into a remarkable, and meaningful, underwater world.

- **Who Hops?,** Katie Davis. Birds fly. Bats fly. Flies fly. Rhinos fly. NO THEY DON'T! Hilarious, with great use of line, borders, and balance as the animals move across the pages (or don't, in the case of the rhino).

- **Zee,** Michel Gay. The baby zebra trying to make breakfast for his parents is clearly drawn, but watercolored in with soft smears that don't fill (and sometimes overlap) the lines. Perfection would mar the charm.

- **Black Meets White,** Justine Fontes, Geoff Waring (illus.). Imagine creating a book about the colors black and white, and making their relationship entertaining and instructive. The final interactive pull-tab is a stroke of genius.

- **Ten Black Dots,** Donald Crews. What can you do with ten black dots? Animals, vegetables, and minerals are all represented. Ten black dots are there too for the counting.

- **That's Good! That's Bad!,** Margery Cuyler, David Catrow (illus.). When a boy at the zoo gets a balloon, that's good. When the balloon carries him away, that's bad—and so on in this wild tale of adventure, illustrated with dramatic close-ups and wide-angle drawings for a lesson in perspective.

- **The Squiggle,** Carole Lexa Schaefer. A found red ribbon becomes a dragon and a thundercloud for a group of imaginative school children. Sparse, simple illustrations become richer in the imagined scenes.

Bringing It All Together

These books are full of images you could hang on the wall.

- ***Big Momma Makes the World,*** Phyllis Root, Helen Oxenbury (illus.). Oxenbury gets an enlarged story to illustrate here, but draws the same bold characters in colorful adventurous activities. It's a great creation myth, as well.

- ***Close Your Eyes,*** Kate Banks, Georg Hallensleben (illus.). Bright watercolors, softly smudged, with few defining lines create a hypnotic bedtime story as a mother tiger reassures her little one about the world of sleep.

- ***George Shrinks,*** William Joyce. Lively, bright, and an amazing adventure in perspective as George tries to complete his chores in spite of being the size of a salt shaker.

- ***Mufaro's Beautiful Daughter,*** John Steptoe. Everything in this African Cinderella story looks realistic and informative, and as personal as if it were a family's artistic scrapbook.

- ***Stone Soup,*** Jon J. Muth. Muth's watercolors pull the reader right into the small Chinese village, where the buildings have almost as much character as the people. The sparse Asian style is a revelation to those used to busy American children's art and eases the transition to a longer—and more abstract—story.

- ***Trouble on the Tracks,*** Kathy Mallat. Markers and colored pencil make for bold artwork, full of hidden clues as to the nature of the "trouble" ahead.

- ***Two Little Trains,*** Margaret Wise Brown, Leo and Diane Dillon (illus.). In the Dillons' first real book for preschoolers, they create dynamic parallels painting a powerful real train and a child's toy train moving along. There is a feeling of motion in a slightly old-fashioned and yet timeless spaciousness.

- ***Frog and Hare,*** Max Velthuijs. THE best Dutch writer-illustrator whose focus on Frog and his friends is simple and reassuringly compassionate. (Plus many more titles translated into at least six different languages: *Frog Is Frightened, Frog in Love, Frog in Winter, Frog Is Frog,* and *Frog and the Birdsong.*)

- ***Polar Bear Night,*** Lauren Thompson, Stephen Savage (illus.). Pastels and soft colors contrast with the defined, linocut style in this story of a baby polar bear's gentle nighttime adventure.

Ages and Stages:
Art Activities with Readers 0–3

Newborn	• Show and Tell: She'll watch and listen whatever you show and tell. • Show: Draw some good fat lines with a marker or crayon. • Talk: Talk about colors, shapes, and pictures or anything else you see.
Heads Up	• She might be able to hold a fat crayon, although unable to do much with it. Help her to make a mark. • Talk about the colors of the things she's holding close. • Give her colored paper to crumple.

Sitting	• Smearing food might lead to finger paints, or just a mess. She might (like KJ's Sam) have hysterics over her dirty hand. • Make a handprint in clay or Play-Doh. • Make or buy large shape magnets for the refrigerator or a metal door. Try to make sure they're easy to pull off and on!
Crawling/Creeping	• Cut a series of objects in a single color out of magazines and tape them onto cards for added sturdiness. Hand her a series of blue objects to look at and hear about! (If you do several colors and the cards survive, later you can mix them up, lay them out, and use them for "pick something blue.") • Invent a point-to or choose-a-shape game.
Cruising/Walking	• Play a color-match game with a book. Try one that's focused on color, like one with a different color on every page. Give her a few (two or three) colored squares to choose from and see if he can make a match. • Make some Play-Doh. Break off some of the flour-white lump and add drops of food dye to create blue, red, yellow, and green balls. • Draw big shapes on paper that you can lay on the ground and help her to stand inside the triangle, the circle, or the square. • Draw lines in the sand, lines in the dirt, lines in the snow, and use sticks, fingers, or feet.

Talking (a few words)	• She'll love watching YOU try to draw in the style of a favorite book or character. Get the book out and try to come up with a simple but recognizable Max or Clifford, and let her color the results. • Straws or pretzel sticks can make a line on the ground or along the table—a line, or a path, or a road. • Play a version of I Spy to spot a color or shape, like where's the red book or where's the round book?
Talking More	• With (a lot of) your help, she can make a collage caterpillar like the very hungry one. Cut out circles for her and stick double-sided tape on the back. Show her how they can overlap to form a caterpillar (and draw in eyes and antennae for her). • Make "puppets" to act out a simple story. You cut out the shape (fish are nice and simple) and make stripes or dots with paper and double-sided tape for her to stick on. Then tape a straw to the back, leaving enough sticking out at the bottom to hold. • Try drawing something she commonly requests, but leave the shape incomplete—a train with a gap in it—and see what she notices. • Squeezable icing is good for drawing. Don't bother with a too-hard-to-squeeze decorative tip. Just take the cap off and squeeze it onto graham crackers. Edible art. • Playfully change the colors of ordinary objects and see what happens. Draw pictures of the snowman in blue, or the refrigerator green, or the dachshund pink.

Running (but not talking much)	• Let the artist stand up. Tape the paper to a wall or easel.
	• Weather permitting, take the activities and chalks outdoors.
	• Gather a ball and a few small cars you don't mind getting dirty, and let her roll them through paint on paper and look at the lines that result.
	• Play "go get the circle/square/triangle" with shapes you've made or found. Vary it by making them in different colors and asking for the red triangle, or the blue circle.
Talking ALL THE TIME!	• Have her dictate a story to you. Then one or both of you draw and color the pictures. Write out her words exactly and then punch holes in the book and tie it together with yarn.
	• Get a new picture book, and have her tell you the story from reading the pictures. Write it down and read it back to her.
	• Talk a little about style—this artist used paper to make these pictures, this one drew, this one painted. When she draws or paints or pastes paper, remind her of favorite books where the technique is the same.
	• Have a "shape meal." Cut sandwiches into circles, serve wagon wheel pasta, round cookies, etc. A variant could be to have a "color clothes day."
	• Play color-spotters anywhere and everywhere. Ask her what color things are now, before she has a firm idea of what color they SHOULD be. The sky may be white or gray today, and the grass blue. Take a look—she's probably right.
	• Using balloon stickers, she can draw the strings. Using train stickers, she can draw a line for the track and another for the smoke.

Chapter Six:
Interactive Books Make Reading "Sensational"

Babies "read" with their eyes, mouth, nose, fingers, and ears. Interactive books put a sensory-filled world easily within baby's grasp. Reading any book is an interactive experience. Nothing happens until you turn the pages. Interactive books dramatically emphasize this. Their textures, flaps, pop-ups, and pull-tabs offer children a chance to reach in and physically engage with them. For babies, the activities are simple: touch the cloth puppy, lift the flap, look in the mirror, feel the bumpy rubber corner with finger or tongue. This is truly the beginning of reading, and it's fun. Toddlers and twos get wheels to spin and tabs to pull. Pages come in different shapes and sizes or with holes revealing a glimpse of what comes next. Pop-ups in their simplest form can work for an older baby and then, becoming gradually more complex, delight all ages. Some books are devoted entirely to touchable textures or pop-up surprises, but many combine all of these elements for a fully three-dimensional experience. Interactive books are usually favorites for every age.

Hard-Working Books for Hard-Working Babies

The importance of touch and feel to an infant cannot be overemphasized. Being held, stroked, snuggled, and swaddled helps her feel secure and valued. Touching, for her, is also an act of discovery. She can use her own sense of touch to explore everything else that's out there. As soon as she can see it, she's going to want to touch it. Have you ever seen a baby trying to pick the paisleys up off of a bedspread? One of the ways she learns that the apple on the page isn't real is by putting out her hand.

Interactive books for baby may feature textures to feel, flaps to lift, or they may be made from cloth, rubber, foam or plastic instead of paper or board. All help to engage the senses of a baby who's used to relying only on sight and sound.

If It's Not Paper, It Won't Rip

There are plenty of books out there that invite your baby's touch. Cloth books offer something soft to touch. Rubber, plastic, and foam are often waterproof and certainly saliva- and chew-proof. All are good additions to a baby's world. Unlike stiff cardboard-paged board books, these books (especially cloth ones) can be floppy, and sometimes hard to read. But they are useful.

One advantage to cloth books is that they last forever. A friend brought Susan a Michigan flea market treasure: a one-hundred-year-old cloth book manufactured in 1905 by Dean's Rag Books. The logo shows two dogs tearing away at the book, with the phrase "Quite Indestructible" underneath the tug-of-war. The images are still wonderfully clear after over a century and the alphabet connections are full of story and poetry, although today's author might replace "G was a gamester who had but ill luck" or "U was an usher who loved little boys" with something a bit more politically correct.

Cloth books are lightweight and easy for a baby to manipulate, and their soft format makes them nearly as cuddly as a favorite animal or blankie. They're great for distracting your baby on the changing pad or table. You'll see her wave the book about, "talk" to it, and perhaps even try to get it into her mouth to taste whether it's a good read or not. Anyone who's seen a baby grab a book and accidentally stick the corner into her eye can see the advantages of cloth. But these books are among the most limited in terms of age range. Few will hold an older child's interest for long.

Books made from other textures like rubber, foam, or plastic may become toy-like and often have a tub theme. Floating plastic tub books are great for a wider range of ages. Foam books, like the Soft Shapes books from Innovative KIDS, usually have pieces to take out and work even better for older babies than very young ones. The pieces can become toys to act out the stories (there's even a train with tracks), or stick to tub walls. Try to put the pieces back in after every reading, or eventually there will be nothing left to read with.

Look Mom, No Paper!
Five Cloth, Plastic, and Foam Favorites

Since the availability of specific titles changes regularly, you may find a different selection at your bookstore. Just look for something you think you and your baby will enjoy.

1. **Sweet, Sweet Baby!,** Javaka Steptoe (illus.). Some text on cloth pages, bordered with noise-making petals, and a mirror.

2. **Spot,** Eric Hill. The loveable puppy comes in all textures, including cloth and plastic for bathtime fun.

3. **Rough Road,** by Kate Davis, Bob Filipowich. All of the Soft Shapes books have sturdy synthetic shapes that punch out like puzzle pieces for lots of playful uses. This one includes four trucks that pop out of four textured roads.

4. **The Lily-Pad Race,** Simon Morse (illus.). Each thick, floatable story page includes a pop-out lily pad or frog, ready to build and play with.

5. **Zoo Faces (Cuddly Cloth),** Willabel L. Tong. Colorful zoo animals offer different textures for babies to stroke, touch, or press against.

Fuzzy Wuzzy Was a Book: Textures to Touch and Feel

Dragging your new baby's hand across a "bunny's" fur or a "chick's" feathers is a lovely feeling for you both. Each fur or feathery swatch prompts you to say something about it. What does it feel like? What do you tell your baby as she comes in contact with the velvety patch that stands for a cow's lips? A little piece of sandpaper that represents Daddy's scratchy face? A small rubbery bit that feels like a tractor's tire?

You can find "touch and feel" books where the texture is inset into a page or glued on, or with textures sticking off of the sides like tags. Foam books may come with different textures to rub. Any of these will probably serve to grab your baby's attention.

Many cloth books come with a hole or ring for attaching to the stroller, and there are some board books with clips attached. These are great for baby to look at on the go, and allow you to jump in with a little reading at odd moments throughout the day.

Babies love touch and feel books because they add another sensory element to reading. Parents love them because they give a busy baby something to do with her hands besides grabbing or pounding on the book you're holding! The best of these blend in the texture with the other art on the page.

Five Fuzzy, Furry, Rough, and Smooth Books for Sticky Fingers

1. ***Touch and Feel: Farm,*** Dorling Kindersley Publishing. All of the titles in this wonderful chunky board book series work for us. Good sturdy choices include *Clothes, Wild Animals,* and *Home.* (Also *Touch and Feel: Birthday* and *Touch and Feel: Mealtime.*)

2. ***Tails,*** Matthew Van Fleet. Animals here have wonderful large and small tails to touch, feel, slide, and flip.

3. ***Are You Ticklish?,*** Sam McKendry, Melanie Mitchell (illus.), Laurie Young (designer). If these textured monkeys, zebras, and elephants are ticklish, are you?

4. ***That's Not My Bunny: Its Tail Is Too Fluffy,*** Fiona Watt, Rachel Wells (illus.). Nice artwork and mini-story in a wonderful series of gentle touch and feels.

5. ***Tickle Teddy: A Touch-and-Feel Book,*** David Ellwand. This sturdy board book has photos of stuffed animals with textured fabric swatches ready for tickling. The baby is next.

Tote That Book, Lift That Flap

The simplest, most straightforward interactive book for a baby or younger toddler is the lift-the-flap. The flaps are an extension of peek-a-boo, the most congenial and universal game. Babies want to know what's in, under, or behind there. Their curiosity makes them want to know what's inside everything, whether it's a paper bag, closet door, or cat litter box. You can play peek-a-boo with any book, of course, opening and shutting its pages, but the flaps invite baby to experiment on her own.

Lift-the-flap books are also excellent conversation pieces. While your baby lifts flaps to help Spot look for his doggie bowl, you can talk with her about her guesses, and her predictions. We love looking for Spot, especially when there's a surprise animal under the flap, like the penguin that answers "NO, he's not here. Try over there." How surreal. How funny. And how entertaining for a fifteen- to eighteen-month-old child who delights in saying "no" herself. Once the animal or object is found, there's no end to the discussion you can have with very little toddlers about it. These discussions, which allow the child to become a teller of the story, are an early form of what academics call Dialogic Reading, one of the cornerstones of literacy.

You'll Never Find a Used Copy of *Pat the Bunny* (Here's Why)

Pat the Bunny by Dorothy Kunhardt, may not have been the first activity book for babies, but it's surely the most enduring. As popular today as when it was first published in 1940, the book appears in almost every baby's new library. What's so great about it? Why is it irresistible?

There they are, Paul and Judy, two old fashioned children who can DO things. Judy can pat the bunny, play peekaboo, look in the mirror, feel Daddy's scratchy face, read her book, and wave bye-bye. Paul can smell the flowers and put his finger through Mummy's ring. All of these activities are in line with a baby's natural development. Best of all, Paul and Judy invite the baby to join them, to try it too, to have fun. Babies touch everything and develop the capacity to grab and hold things, like the books we're holding—and here is Judy's book, waiting to be seized. They crave applause, approval, and the bunny in Judy's book teaches them a winning trick. "How big is bunny?" "Soooooooooo big!" Bunny gestures outwards with his ears and arms. "How big is baby?" a parent asks. "Soooo big!" gestures baby stretching her arms wide, too. Applause. Delight. Again.

Real babies face a steady stream of people coming and going to attend to their needs, some of whom wave and say bye-bye. After smiling, waving bye-bye is one of baby's first sociable acts, and Paul and Judy wave bye-bye too, but they can be brought back with just a flip of the page. Is there an element of nostalgia in *Pat the Bunny*'s continuing popularity? Of course. But your affection for it isn't what pulls out Judy's book, rips Mummy's ring, and yanks the peekaboo cloth right off of Paul. That's baby's job—and she's good at it. If she loves it to death, you may have to buy another copy.

Nine Books of Flaps for Lifting

1. **Dear Zoo: A Lift-the-Flap Book,** Rod Campbell. When a child writes to the zoo to request a pet, a series of animals are sent, flaps are opened, and creatures are rejected as too big, too tall, too fierce, until the perfect pet arrives. It's great fun.

2. **Where Is Maisy?,** Lucy Cousins. Maisy is bright, simple, and charming, and Cousin's questioning flaps invite answers.

3. **Whose Feet? Whose Ears? Whose Nose?,** Jeannette Rowe. Questions are posed and answers are found partially hidden under flaps that all end with my feet, ears, or nose.

4. **Feed the Animals, See the Circus, Where's My Baby?,** and **How Do You Get There?,** H. A. Rey. From the creator of *Curious George*, these simple lift-the-flap books have been entertaining babies for at least two generations. Because they're paper rather than board, they're not necessarily the sturdiest, but full of narrative and joy.

5. **Fuzzy Yellow Ducklings,** Matthew Van Fleet. A nice combination of touchable textures and lift-the-flaps.

6. **Baby's Box of Fun : A Karen Katz Lift-the-Flap Gift Set: Where Is Baby's Belly Button?; Where Is Baby's Mommy?; Toes, Ears, & Nose (Box Set),** Karen Katz, Marion Dane Bauer. Bestseller stuff for babies and toddlers because they are well constructed, entertaining, and lead directly to knowing body parts like belly button, toes and nose.

7. **Where Is Humpty Dumpty?** Harriet Ziefert, Laura Rader (and *What Happened to Jack and Jill?*). Wonderful combinations of two flaps per page to answer the nursery rhymed riddles. Brief and fun.

8. **ABC Look at Me!,** Roberta Intrater. Each letter opens up to an adorable baby face expressing the feeling or fun, like R is for Rowdy when I'm fooling around; and O is for Ouch when I get a boo-boo.

9. **Grandma, Where Are You?** Harriet Ziefert, Emilie Boon (illus.). A hippo child searches for his granny in the garden and the bath, then has her find him. Very cute.

Paper Engineering:
Pulls, Pop-ups, and Whirl-a-ma-jigs for Toddlers and Up

Interactive books for toddlers and twos require even more participation of the reader. He must figure out what's expected—pull the tab? Push it? Move it around on the page? Wheels and pulls and levers beg to be touched or tugged. Paper pop-up structures burst from the page. Just as they do the younger baby, books that engage multiple senses draw the older baby or toddler in and make reading even more of an adventure.

{ *"I'm reading to my nephew of eleven months every opportunity I get. He has specific favorites even now. One of them is a lift-the-flap Maisy book. Now when he reads a regular board book, he grabs at the pages searching for the flap."* —Rachel }

Tabs and Tugs for Busy Fingers

Books with tabs to pull, wheels to turn, or paper levers to shift are ideal for the curious toddler or two-year-old. Even more than pop-ups, these books, like lift-the-flaps, require reader interaction. Some allow the child to help enact the words on the page, some address the child directly, asking for help that can only be provided by the nimble-fingered reader. Moving the outstretched tab makes the windshield wipers move, lifting the flap moves a passenger in and out of the bus door. It's like magic.

These books offer the excitement of making something happen and provide bonus lessons in the areas of manual dexterity and patience. The tabs and wheels can be frustratingly difficult at first and then too floppy to have much effect unless they're handled just right. The desire to get it right is so strong, the risks—a ripped book, a bent page—bearable, but still there. It makes the book and the reading experience just a little more special when there's something at stake, however small it may seem to you. Maybe because they're almost like toys, maybe just because they're full of thrills and surprises, these books are often favorites and reading them even more of a treat.

Books to Engage Nimble Fingers

- **The Elmer Pop-Up Book,** David McKee. Flaps, pulls, and lots of movement starring the multicolored, checkerboard elephant Elmer.

- **We're Going on an Airplane!,** Steve Augarde. Lots of aviation activities, perfect for a trip or just an airplane fan.

- **The Wheels on the Bus,** Paul O. Zelinsky. The wipers swish. The doors open and shut, the people go up and down, the babies go wah, wah, wah. One of the best interactive books out there to date.

- **Knick-Knack Paddywhack,** Paul O. Zelinsky. Another interactive song with plenty of details and fun movement.

- **Maisy's ABC,** Lucy Cousins. A flap to lift or a tag to pull for every letter.

- **Peek-a-Zoo,** Marie Torres Cimarusti, Stephanie Peterson (illus.). Animal peek-a-boo, with nice big baby-sized faces.

- **If You're Happy and You Know It,** David A. Carter. Happy animals clap hands, wag tails, etc. as you sing along.

- **Farm Animals (Magic Color Book),** Louisa Sladen, Luana Rinaldo (illus.). Pull the heavy, thick tabs to help the farm animals reveal their colors.

Boo! Pop-ups to Startle, Tickle, and Thrill

Pop-ups, unlike pulls, flaps, and twirls, happen automatically when you open the book or turn the page. The image pops up. It jumps out of the book's pages at you or towards you. Depending on what pops up, these books can be very funny or even very scary. There's a bit of the charm of the unexpected—most books stay flat, after all—which makes a pop-up book just a little more exciting.

There is no sob louder than that of an older child whose pop-up has been ripped out by the baby, unless it's the baby when the older child won't let her have the pop-up book. Try designating a few special pop-ups for the older child alone. When the inevitable disaster strikes, involving her in the repair work may dry her tears.

Pop-ups range from the simple and relatively solid work of the Snappy series to the intricate spinning fantasies of Robert Sabuda. They may seem a little less participatory, but it's the page turn that makes it happen. One result of a pop-up surprise could be a scream from the baby. On the second reading, the anticipation of the page turn is like the baby version of a horror movie, where organ music crescendos signal the approach of a creeping, crawling thing. For some kids, this might be too much. For others, it's great to do it again and again, a monster well within their control.

A set of interactive books makes a great welcome gift for a second or third baby. Send a simple book, like *That's Not My Puppy: Its Coat Is Too Hairy,* for the new baby and appropriate books for the children already in residence, like Paul Zelinsky's *The Wheels on the Bus* for a toddler or a two and a Robert Sabuda pop-up fantasy for an older child. These are gifts the whole family can enjoy for years to come.

Q: What about books pleases babies?

A: I think babies may enjoy a very wide range of things, including books you might think are much too old for them. Little babies are so busy cataloging the world around them, so to speak, that they're not ready for the kind of understanding that story requires. The difference between a good story and a bad story probably escapes a baby; instead, it's all about things, and the qualities of things—the findable details, the sensual pleasure in color and texture, and so on. I don't think this means that a good story ruins a book for a baby, and it certainly helps out whoever is doing the reading.

I know that *The Wheels on the Bus* has been loved by large numbers of babies as well as older children. Little subplots in the pictures make it more interesting for older readers. Perhaps they also add to the number of subjects for a baby to look at and get involved in: a box of kittens; a lady on a motorcycle; a tiny girl in a window looking at you through binoculars.

Q. What do you remember about reading to your two daughters?

A: Both of my daughters loved to have books read to them as babies, but they went about it in such different ways. Anna, the older one, would sit on a lap in rapt attention, even as a tiny infant, and soak up the experience. Rachel, in the same situation four years later, would have to reach out and grab the book, and then chew on it. At that point we started stocking up on more board books.

Anna had a favorite book for several long months that drove us up a wall. It was a board book with a clock on its cover, featuring movable hands. Inside, the book showed a boy and a girl telling a cursory story of their day—breakfast, lunch, visiting a favorite aunt—all at certain times on the clock, illustrated by photographs of cloth dolls in dollhouse settings.

The text was painfully, even ridiculously, dull, not to mention ungrammatical—it was a bad translation from what I suppose was at least correct Japanese. And Anna loved it. I assume she did because the pictures were sharp, close-up, intensely real images of cute dolls. She wasn't especially interested in the movable clock on the cover. After a while, of course, she knew it by heart, and would "read" it out loud, in all its grammatical oddness, as she paged through it, even though she might be holding it upside down, or turning pages from back to front.

Q: Did you remember books from your own childhood?

A: Once I was reading Anna a Babar book borrowed from the library, and I was startled by a strange memory. Suddenly I saw the spread I was reading from, in a memory that I dimly recalled from a very young age. In memory, the picture looked the same and yet very different. It showed the monkey Zephir's hometown, a village made of tree houses all interlaced with rope ladders and bridges. The picture before my adult eyes was nice, slightly abstract, and a bit crudely drawn. The picture I remembered was a thousand times more detailed, realistic, and (I have to say it) more wonderful. For a while I felt as if I were looking at a double exposure, these two not-quite-matching versions of the same image. I thought about this for a long time afterwards, how richly my young eyes interpreted that sparely presented scene. It was like looking at a semi-abstract painting and seeing a photograph. What's amazing is how much of my own imagination was involved in my perception of someone else's image. It makes me wish I could have a peek inside the brain of children looking at my picture books.

Pop-ups to Love

- **Bugs in Space,** David A. Carter. Bug Rogers travels in a bug- and pun-filled outer space. Part of a series (*Birthday Bugs, Alphabet Bugs, Halloween Bugs,* etc.) that includes pop-ups, envelopes to open, even masks to wear.

- **Cookie Count,** Robert Sabuda. A simple counting book by the master of pop-ups. His art in *The Wizard of Oz* and *Alice in Wonderland* is probably too intricate for any but the most careful of two-year-olds, but this serves as a great introduction to his work.

- **Truck Jam,** Paul Stickland. Great big trucks pop out of every page.

- **Monkey Business,** Paul Stickland. A monkey introduces pop-up jungle friends to the newest member of his family.

- **Dinner Time,** Jan Piénkowski. Hungry animals pop-up and chow down in a great starter pop-up from a popular and playful artist.

Someone Cut a Hole in the Page!

Among the many ways to add texture and dimension to a book page is to cut out a piece, so that a glimpse of the next page is revealed. Pages of increasing size may gradually reveal a whole picture, as Eric Carle does in *The Very Hungry Caterpillar,* where each increasingly larger page shows the caterpillar eating yet another thing. Or the cut-outs may combine to create a wholly different picture than each page offers on its own. Ed Emberley uses this technique brilliantly on *Go Away, Big Green Monster.* The monster starts out as just a pair of eyes, then each successive page adds a new scary feature. After the monster is complete, the fangs, hair, etc., are removed, one by one. It's great for putting children in charge of their fear.

Cut-out holes can also be used to emphasize shapes and colors, or to hint at the answer to a question. Many young children love these books because they also give them a new (and sometimes easier) way to turn the page—by reaching right into the hole. Mostly, though, like lift-the-flaps, they add an element of peekaboo to reading. These books, a little more complex, will probably last a little longer.

Holey Page-Turners, Batkid!

- **There Was an Old Lady Who Swallowed a Fly,** Simms Taback. Die-cut pages reveal all that the old lady swallows as the reader sings along.

- **Lemons Are Not Red,** Laura Vaccaro Seeger. Cutouts give clues to the right color of lemons, carrots, and apples, with clever surprises tucked in too.

- **Peek-a-Who,** Nina Laden. Peek-a-boo holes hint at what's coming in a sturdy board book with a mirror ending for the final "Peek-a-You!"

- **Too Many Bunnies,** Matt Novak. Turning these pages makes a family of bunnies "hop" from one hole to another, until their first hole is empty and the new hole is full.

- **Ten Little Ladybugs,** Melanie Gerth, Tony Griego (illus.). Count down these ten touchable ladybugs that appear through the holes on each page.

- **Miffy's Magnifying Glass,** Dick Bruna. Miffy examines various animals up close using her magnifying glass, a large round hole, to focus.

Prepare for Repairs

The mechanics of these more complex activity books are part of the fun. At first, the flaps will be pulled off and the pop-ups torn through sheer enthusiasm. Later, it may be the urge to figure out why pulling the tab opens the door to the bus that leads to the page being torn open and the magic destroyed. Take a deep breath and dry the tears. It's only a book and it doesn't seem quite right to punish a child for enjoying a book too much. Most damage can be repaired, and the space bug will live to pop out of the moon another day. If it's possible, include your child in the repair process. Helping to fix the mistake helps her deal with her upset feelings. It will also reassure her that she hasn't ruined the book forever.

A supply of tape, plain and double-sided, can work wonders. If a moving piece has been pulled off, limit your taping to the piece itself and the fragment remaining—try to keep the tape off the page, and as thin as possible, especially if the piece needs to fit down into a pocket. Push and pull tabs can be reinforced with new cardboard. In many books, the engineering is hidden inside the page (two pages folded or glued together). You may have to perform open-page surgery to give your patient a new (probably temporary) lease on life.

The Toy-Book Continuum

When is a book a book, and when is a book a toy? Sometimes books come packaged with a toy, and sometimes the books are the toy. There are books with wheels, books with removable parts for making a doll or a train, books with movable parts attached by strings and books that form a house for a removable paper mouse. Are those really books at all?

> *"My almost-three-year-old daughter had an animal/alphabet pop-up book which she has recently rediscovered. It's not quite the book it once was, but she still likes it. Now we read it like this:*
>
> *Samantha: H is for...what's that?*
>
> *Me: It used to be a hippo.*
>
> *Samantha: Oh. P is for...what's that?*
>
> *Me: It used to be a parrot."*
>
> —*Jennifer*

All books are invitations to enter a new place, even books hidden within toy purses and tractors. Books contain possibilities for fun and learning. Some small children use their books as toys even though they are "just books." They stack books and knock them down. It's all creative play. Think back to the real reason you want to read with your child—so that reading will be fun. If the wheels on the book have to go round and round, so be it.

> *"I watched a parent in a bookstore recently with an older girl, around seven, who'd evidently been told she could buy any book she wanted. She kept returning to her father with a doll/book combo, a little purse with a book attached, and so on, and her father kept reminding her, 'A book. I said a book, not a toy.' They both left disappointed, a lesson in mismatched expectations."* —*KJ*

IRRESISTIBLE AUTHORS	DAVID A. CARTER

From his *Bugs* books, like *Feely Bugs*, *Birthday Bugs*, and holiday-themed *Bugs That Go Bump in the Night* and *Jingle Bugs* to books like *Old MacDonald Had a Farm (A Pop-Up Book)* and even (for older children) *Elements of Pop-Up: A Pop-Up Book for Aspiring Paper Engineers*, Carter's colorful, innovative works of paper artistry offer something to all ages, from the baby just learning to tug the feathers on the page to the grown-up chuckling at the spiral eyes of the bug those feathers are glued on. Although the books are paper rather than board, they are sturdy enough to hold up to repeated rough readings. These are books you will find your child huddled over, turning the pages for himself, or that he will bring to you again and again.

Twenty-Eight Especially Engaging, Incredible Interactive Books

For Babies and Up:

1. ***Snappy Little Jungle: Have a Wild Time,*** Dugald Steer, Derek Matthews (illus.). Sturdy, brightly colored moving pop-ups illustrate all the books in this fun series.

2. ***There Was an Old Woman Who Swallowed a Fly,*** Jan Piénkowski. Each animal the old woman swallows leaps off the page, full of movement, to the delight of little children everywhere—and no punches are pulled with this traditional rhyme. What happened to the old woman who swallowed a horse? She died, of course.

3. ***Sweet Dreams, Sam,*** Yves Got. It's time for bed, little Sam! But which plush animal friend should he take to bed with him? There's soft furry tiger, fuzzy felt monkey, or rough and scratchy crocodile.

4. Where's Sam?, Yves Got. Lovely big flaps hide one of our favorite bunnies.

5. Animal Kisses, Barney Saltzberg. A touch-and-feel book introducing words which name textures like scratchy cat kisses. Or do you prefer squeaky pig kisses? Or a velvety cow kiss?

6. Happy Baby: It's Your Bedtime, Roger Priddy. Die-cut heads of photographed babies with simple pre-bed things, ending with a mirror to fit your baby right into the book.

7. My Daddy, Matthew Price, Jean Claverie (illus.). As a little boy describes his daddy, readers lift the half-flaps which cover every page to see the picture evolve.

8. One Yellow Lion, Matthew Van Fleet. Opening the flaps shows each large number becoming part of the animals depicted, all frolicking on the page and ready for counting. A final accordion pull-out reveals all the animals together.

9. Inside Freight Train, Donald Crews. Slide the page open to see what's inside the railroad cars.

10. Who Took the Cookie from the Cookie Jar?, David A. Carter. Animals and nicely decorated cookie jars.

11. Fuzzy Yellow Ducklings, Matthew Van Fleet. Lift the flaps to answer the ducky questions.

12. Tap, Tap! Who's There?, Karen Jones. The rare interactive book that works for babies but goes beyond flaps and textures, this tiny board book has a hole for baby to put a finger in and slide up the answer to the titular question. (Also *Munch Munch!*)

13. Where Is Baby's Belly Button?, Karen Katz. Where are baby's hands? Under the bubbles! Where are baby's eyes? Under her hat! Karen Katz's adorable babies play peek-a-boo in this sturdy easy-to-lift flap book.

14. **Opposites,** Robert Crowther. Pushing, sliding, pulling these tabs features new and old opposites like full and empty, off and on, and above and below. Wonderful colors too.

15. **Buzzy's Birthday,** Harriet Ziefert, Emily Bolam. This lift-the-flap edition focuses on the dilemma of waiting patiently for the big day to arrive.

16. **What in the World?,** Eve Merriam, Barbara J. Phillips-Duke (illus.). Delightfully flowing word riddles offer a rich guessing game. Just lift the flaps to find the answers.

17. **Animal Popposites,** Matthew Reinhart. Lift the colorful flap, framed by the white page, to see the pop-up illustrations to opposites like dark and bright.

18. **Charlie the Chicken,** Nick Denchfield and Ant Parker. This chicken eats a lot so he'll grow up big and strong—like his (really big) mama!

19. **Woof-Woof,** SAMi (that's actually how you spell his name). These foam-filled pages morph with a flip of the page into another animal that makes a new noise. Graphically perfect for babies. (Also *Baby Animals* and *Baby Talk* with Harriet Ziefert.)

20. **Yum! and GO!,** SAMi. As the page turns, a piece of pizza becomes an ice cream cone, a tractor turns into a boat. Shapes are emphasized in an entertaining context.

For Nimble Toddlers, Two- and Three-Year-Olds:

21. **I Can Do It!,** Oshkosh. Children can practice how to buckle a belt, set the table, brush their teeth, and tie a bow—all by themselves! This fun-filled and educational book includes safe, child-friendly attachments on each soft cloth page and the Oshkosh seal of approval. (Also *How to Get Dressed*.)

22. _10 Button Book,_ William Accorsi. Ten safety-tested buttons hang off this double-sized board book, ready for pushing into the colorful button sized holes on every page.

23. _My Granny's Purse,_ Paul Hanson. Almost more of a toy than a book, this board creation actually is a purse, with many little purse items and a tiny story inside.

24. _Take Me Out to the Ball Game,_ Jack Norworth, John Stadler (illus.). The classic lyrics, combined with pop-ups and pulls that let the reader in on the game.

25. _The House That Mack Built,_ Susanna Leonard Hill, Ken Wilson-Max (illus.). The classic cumulative story with pop-up construction trucks and more.

For Careful Preschoolers and Up (and Their Delighted Parents):

26. _Alice's Adventures in Wonderland, The Wizard of Oz,_ Robert Sabuda. The classic stories, somewhat abridged, with the classic illustrations brilliantly rendered as pop-up art. Many three-year-olds will be able to sit still for the stories (maybe with a little additional abridgment by the reader) with such amazing creations to look at.

27. _Encyclopedia Prehistorica: Dinosaurs,_ Robert Sabuda and Matthew Reinhart. Although a little short on actual information about dinosaurs, the wonderful pop-ups (created by Saubuda from art by Reinhart) will still delight fans. Toddlers and preschoolers will be as fascinated as older children, although only you can judge whether your child will be able to control the urge to grab. Probably a good book to keep on a high shelf.

28. _One Red Dot,_ David A. Carter. Find the red dot hidden in each elaborate paper sculpture.

Chapter Seven:
Nursery Rhymes, Poetry, Songs, and Fingerplay

Both babies and adults love music, rhyme, and rhythm. It's a kind of default setting for grown-ups: your mind sees a baby and immediately offers up nursery rhymes, songs, and fingerplays. If you haven't already started singing whatever pops into your head, and noticing how quickly your baby responds, you probably will soon. Many a grandmother, tucked in next to the baby's car seat, has made a long drive go by in the blink of an eye with the repeated toe touches of "This Little Piggy Went to Market." (Of course, the ride may have felt longer to everyone else in the car, but we've never known a baby who didn't love Piggy even more the sixtieth time around.)

These categories overlap. Some nursery rhymes are songs. Some have finger or hand motions. Sometimes you're not entirely sure where that half-remembered couplet came from, but it doesn't matter. The charm, for both you and baby, lies in the irresistible rhythms, the catchy tunes, and the universal appeal. These little rhymes and games have their roots deep in our culture. Our mothers tickled our wee little piggies, their mothers ticked theirs. Now it's our turn to be the tickler. Time to pass it along.

Nursery Rhymes

All of us, newborn and old and everything in between, love nursery rhymes. It doesn't matter if we learn at our mother's knee or from our preschool class or caregiver, Mother Goose stays with us forever. Because nursery rhymes are so compelling, they can be a wonderfully effective form of shared connection. The rhymes, and in some cases the tunes, make them easy to remember. Babies learn them quickly, and nothing delights a parent more than to see that her baby is learning. As soon as he responds to the rhyme with the right word or gesture, the baby can get a big reaction from his caregiver—and he'll want to see the same reaction again.

Once your toddler can recite "Hey Diddle Diddle," get out the tape recorder or video camera. He may refuse to perform, but if you can capture his rendition, complete with pauses and explanations, you'll have a real treasure.

Knowing nursery rhymes is key to future connections and fun. He'll hear the same rhyme again at school, do the same hand motions with his caregivers, and even play the game on the playground, instantly accompanied by the equally well-educated kids around him. Nursery rhymes are one of the few reliable shared pieces of our culture. With a few nursery rhymes under his belt, your baby is prepared for all kinds of things. Once he's learned one, the rest come even more easily. He's expanding his memory and his horizons all at once.

Once Upon a History Lesson

Once upon a time, these nursery rhymes actually taught, or at least mocked, a little piece of history.

Humpty Dumpty sat on a wall.
Humpty Dumpty had a great fall.
All the king's horses and all the king's men
Couldn't put Humpty together again!

Humpty Dumpty was a powerful cannon during the English Civil War (1642–1649), mounted on top of a great church. While the Royalists were defending the city against siege in the summer of 1648, the church tower was hit by the enemy and the top of the tower was blown off, sending "Humpty" tumbling to the ground. Naturally the king's horses (cavalry) and men (infantry) tried to mend him, but in vain.

Ironically, the rhymes survive where often the history does not. Linguists still debate whether "Ring around the Rosy" refers back to the Bubonic Plague (the consensus seems to be that it does not), but agree that "Old King Cole" probably had its roots in an early Celtic ruler. Apparently, the power of nursery rhymes to attract and enchant lasts well into graduate school.

Growing Up with Mother Goose and Friends

Nursery rhymes work at every stage, from babies to toddlers to twos. Babies are learning the charm and power of repetition. They'll appreciate the growing familiarity of the rhymes, recited with or without a book and accompanying illustrations. If there are exhilarating or stimulating gestures that go along with a rhyme, like a bump up into the air or a sudden tickle, they will quickly learn to anticipate the joyous payoff.

> *"I was just floored when I was reading along in our Mother Goose book and I got to the end of 'The Old Woman Who Lived in a Shoe.' Did you remember that she 'whipped them all soundly and put them to bed'? I'm actually just waiting for him to be old enough to ask what 'whipped' means."* —Beth

As they grow older, a familiar rhyme can give them a chance to show off new words and new skills. A talking toddler can fill in "Hey diddle diddle, the cat and the fiddle, the cow jumped over the…moon." He can raise his arms to show the sun coming out in "Eensy Weensy Spider," and pat-a-cake awkwardly along with the baker's man.

At two, his growing sense of humor may appreciate an unexpected twist in the familiar (the more ridiculous, the better): when she got there, the cupboard was bare, and so the poor dog had…macaroni and cheese! The hand gestures will become more accurate, the tunes somewhat less wavering. Many kids will be able to recite a surprising number of rhymes with little prompting before their third birthday, and will recognize a new book with a familiar rhyme instantly. Even better, he can "read" a well-known rhyme from a brand-new book by following the illustrations.

Nursery Rhyme Collections to Love

- **Richard Scarry's Best Mother Goose Ever,** A big book with fifty favorite rhymes (one per page) and Scarry's classic animal illustrations.

- **Real Mother Goose: My First Mother Goose,** Blanche Fisher Wright. Seven favorites, with old-fashioned illustrations that seem just right, touchable inserts, and a scratch-and-sniff Pat-a-Cake. Also available as a board book.

- **My Mother Goose Library,** (Two volumes: *My Very First Mother Goose and Here Comes Mother Goose),* Iona Archibald Opie (editor), Rosemary Wells (illus.). A mix of rhymes both popular and more obscure in an oversized format, perfect for pressing open and poring over the details of Ms. Wells's instantly recognizable style.

- **The Neighborhood Mother Goose,** Nina Crews. This new and hip collection uses photography to capture real kids in genuine city parks, streets, and houses acting out the rhymes.

- **Mother Goose: A Collection of Classic Nursery Rhymes,** Michael Hague. With a useful index of first lines at the end of this volume, there are plenty of old fashioned-type illustrations of familiar and a few less well-known choice nursery rhymes.

- **Mary Englebreit's Mother Goose: One Hundred Best-Loved Verses,** Mary Englebreit. This collection is really charmingly illustrated, in a slightly toned down version of Englebreit's usual style that works well for kids. It's nearly all-inclusive, with popular favorites, obscure rhymes, and useful bits like "Thirty Days Has September."

- **Animal Crackers: A Delectable Collection of Pictures, Poems, and Lullabies for the Very Young,** Jane Dyer. A short, easy to carry collection of popular rhymes that radiate with Ms. Dyer's artistic talents.

A Mother Goose of His Own

Have you ever pored over a big book of nursery rhymes, studying the illustrations and reminding yourself of the lyrics (perhaps even saying or singing them under your breath)? Some of us were eight or nine when we did it the last time; some of us over fifty. Many famous illustrators have enjoyed putting their own unique stamp on these familiar treasures. Because of its longevity, we urge you to acquire a really good and perhaps expensive edition. The production value of many big nursery rhymes collections is well worth it. Just keep some tape handy to repair inevitable page tears. You can borrow other collections from the library. There are so many examples of excellent illustrated nursery rhymes that inevitably you and your baby will begin to enter the lit crit world of compare and contrast, enhancing the pleasure.

W. W. Denslow, An American Classic

Nursery rhymes themselves are relics of another, nearly forgotten age, with their cupboards and curds and carriages. A collection from the first American picture book illustrator W. W. Denslow is still available in *Denslow's Picture Book Treasury*. (You may recognize his style from *The Wonderful Wizard of Oz* or his curious seahorse signature.) Denslow's illustrations give us the opportunity to see those durable, unchanging little doggerels in the context of another era. As his Old Mother Hubbard rushes about to provide for her pet, we still find it funny to see this shoeless dog with his feet up on a table, wearing a smoking jacket and powdered wig, reading the news. It's a little like watching Shakespeare's *Romeo and Juliet* morph into *West Side Story* and then into *Romeo + Juliet*. The pictures, the costumes, the accessories all give us a new insight into the original story. Times change. Rhymes don't.

Just One Rhyme

Is it worth it to buy a picture book that illustrates just one nursery rhyme? Yes, particularly for babies and toddlers. A single rhyme spread over focused illustrations is perfect, in fact preferable to a more elaborate book.

- **Little Bo Peep,** Tracey Campbell Pearson. The rhyme is classic, but the illustrations show that Bo Peep is a sleepy baby whose sheep has fallen from her crib.

- **Diddle, Diddle, Dumpling,** Tracey Campbell Pearson. There is something about the phrase "one shoe off and one shoe on" that captures kids' imaginations (and comes up constantly in their easily distractible lives). Campbell Pearson's irresistible baby, sound asleep in his lone shoe, charms.

- **Old Mother Hubbard and Her Wonderful Dog,** James Marshall. Marshall extends the rhyme to allow Mother Hubbard even more adventures with her flamboyantly costumed dog. Includes visual jokes for all ages.

- **Mary Had a Little Lamb,** Sarah Josepha Hale, Bruce McMillan (illus.). This version uses photographs to follow Mary, a charming African American girl in glasses and yellow overalls, as she goes off to school. The blend of old-fashioned design with modern details brings this classic rhyme into a new age.

- **Hey, Diddle, Diddle!,** Salley Mavor. Illustrated with photographs of carefully constructed, detailed felt and fabric creations.

- **Pat-A-Cake,** Tony Kenyon. Simple illustrations show the baker playing the familiar clapping game.

- **Fiddle-I-Fee: A Farmyard Song for the Very Young,** Melissa Sweet. A small child feeds animals who all make sounds as this song-rhyme book bounces along. The animals are enchanted, it seems, by the small person and eagerly follow along to a family picnic.

Beyond Mother Goose: Poetry for Babies and Up

Many books for babies rhyme, but not many authors are really writing poetry for this age group. There's a somewhat intangible difference between a book of rhyming descriptions of textured bugs, the fabulous doggerel narratives of Dr. Seuss, and the slightly wistful verse of Shel Silverstein. However, you will find poetry books on a wide range of topics (cats, teddy bears, families, and bathtime) and from the world beyond (India, Russia, China, and Japan). Without lingering too long on what's NOT poetry, we'd like to suggest some books that are.

Poems That Stand Alone

- *Jamberry,* Bruce Degen. A fun and rhythmic listing of real and fanciful berries.

- *Jesse Bear's Wiggle-Jiggle Jump-Up,* Nancy White Carlstrom, Bruce Degen (illus.). A poem with an insistent country-western swing to help a young bear get dressed.

- *Sleepytime Rhyme,* Remy Charlip. A mother reassures her baby with a lullaby that details her love from lip to tippy toe.

- *Is Your Mama a Llama?,* Deborah Guarino. Llama Lloyd asks lots of animal friends if their mamas are llamas.

- *A House Is a House for Me,* Mary Ann Hoberman, Betty Fraser (illus). The rhymes provide lots of wonderful information about homes for animals (a web for a spider) all the way up to people. Full of life and energy.

- **Sheep in a Shop,** Nancy E. Shaw, Margot Apple (illus.). Each book in the series of lambs getting into humorous people-like situations is delightful.

- **Barnyard Dance!,** Sandra Boynton. This energetic, insistent rhythm book for babies has lots of chickens and cows swinging and dancing.

- **Snowmen at Night,** Caralyn Buehner, Mark Buehner (illus.). Ever wonder what snowmen do at night? The Buehners tell the inside scoop in entertaining verse. A great book for sharing among siblings because each illustration includes hidden pictures for an older child to find.

- **Jazz Baby,** Carole Boston Weatherford, Laura Freeman (illus.). The rhythms are an insistent pat-a-cake that make you and your baby interactively move.

{ *"Whenever Gus wants to talk to someone now, he goes up to them, pats them gently on the leg, and asks, 'Is your mama a llama?'"* —Judith }

Poetry Collections

Books of poems written especially for children are typically too grown-up for our age group, created as they are for older ones who are more verbally competent. But the more you nurture very young babies on nursery rhymes, the more they will get poetry later on.

- *Welcome, Baby! Baby Rhymes for Baby Times,* Stephanie Calmenson, Melissa Sweet (illus.). These books contribute simple poems and drawings about things babies and toddlers know well: "Pots and spoons are very good toys," "Silly Toe Song," and "Babies in a Stroller." (Also *Good for You! Toddler Rhymes for Toddler Times.*)

- *Read-Aloud Rhymes for the Very Young,* Jack Prelutsky (editor), Marc Brown (illus.). This collection is probably for older than our under-threes, but since there are multiple images and poems per page, it's a good choice for reading with siblings.

- *Where the Sidewalk Ends,* Shel Silverstein. Although the content of his poetry will appeal more to older children, babies will enjoy his rhythm and preschoolers his nonsense. Try his recipe for a hippo sandwich or dancing pants and for sure his "Ickle Me Pickle Me Tickle Me Too."

- *Sing a Song of Popcorn: Every Child's Book of Poems,* M. White, Ed Moore, B. De Regniers, et al., nine Caldecott illustrators. This is a huge compendium volume of selections brilliantly illustrated by significant, award-winning children's book illustrators. There is something for everyone, and particularly different ages of readers, lookers, and listeners.

- *Now We Are Six,* A. A. Milne, Ernest H. Shepard (illus.). This is a true classic book of poetry for and about childhood. "Half way up the stairs is a stair where I sit," and "James James Morrison Morrison Weatherby George Dupree/Took great care of his mother though he was only three." Can't get better than this.

- **Bedtime Rhymes,** Carol Thompson. Simple, plainly illustrated original short rhymes and riffs on more familiar rhymes, all with a bedtime theme.

- **Arroz con Leche: Popular Songs and Rhymes from Latin America,** Lulu Delacre. All of the poems are written in both English and Spanish, with music at the end, and joyous, colorful pictures to illustrate the sights and sounds and families of Latin America.

- **Las Nanas de Abuelita/Grandmother's Nursery Rhymes,** Nelly Palacio Jaramillo (compiler), Elivia (illus.). "Mommy and Daddy I'd like a chance to marry a girl/Who knows how to dance..." is how it all starts, and shifts easily in and out of Spanish and English, with illustrations of a very loveable granny and kids.

- **¡Pío Peep! Traditional Spanish Nursery Rhymes,** Alma Flor Ada, Vivi Escriva (illus.). So much music comes pouring forth from this well-known classic collection that even those of us who can't sing WILL feel the lilt of these Spanish poems. Aided by English renditions of the familiar Spanish works, we also have kid-friendly fingerplays to try.

- **Sol a Sol, Lori Carlson,** Emily Lisker (illus.). Perhaps technically for older children, but the artwork and familiar activities (cooking) and people (Abuela/Grandma) resonate so vividly that this volume of poems works for all ages.

- **Poetry Speaks to Children,** Elise Paschen (ed.), Judy Love, Wendy Rasmussen, Paula Zinngrabe Wendland (illus.). A brightly illustrated collection of kid-friendly work by poets from Shakespeare to Langston Hughes and modern artists as well. With so much variety (and a CD of poems, many read by the poets), this should serve your family well from infancy into the teen years.

IRRESISTIBLE AUTHOR — DR. SEUSS, A POET WHO KNOWS IT

Dr. Seuss certainly qualifies as a writer of poetic verse for children. His work offers so much pleasure to so many readers and listeners that he may well be a cornerstone for a lifetime of reading. His narratives are like a child's version of *The Iliad* and *The Odyssey*, epic sagas written to be spoken aloud and very decidedly in poetic meter.

Dr. Seuss is for children of all ages. Some of his books are better understood and appreciated by older kids who can follow the funny stories, but *Hop on Pop*, *One Fish*, *Two Fish*, *Red Fish*, *Blue Fish*, and *The Foot Book* all ring the bell. His *Yertle the Turtle* collection of stories, with their heavily accented rhymes, is suitable for all ages, and most assuredly for young ones between eighteen months and three years. The stories are easy to understand although describing complicated human-like dynamics, the illustrations are typically memorable Seuss, and the rhymes are captivating. His drawings, rendered in blue, green, and black on a white background, help children focus on the details being read aloud by the adult reader.

Fingerplay and Action Rhymes

Fingerplay is a combined entertainment for both parents and kids. "Whoops Johnny" and "Where Is Thumbkin" delight again and again.

Do you remember "The Grand Old Duke of York"? Generations of kids have enjoyed this historical rendition of what sounds like a rather futile army exercise. Like most nursery rhymes, it has an historical provenance (it's said to refer to the Duke of York's disastrous decision to march his troops down from their hilltop stronghold and attack during the War of the Roses). It also lends itself to action. Fourteen-month-old Connor and his mother Amy showed us how the Grand Old Duke marched his men up (arms overhead) or down (arms down), and how the arms, like the Duke's men, flailed up and down when they were neither up nor down. Librarian Peggy had her Lapsit Program babies and caregivers play it a little differently. Sitting on the floor, babies held on outstretched legs, her group bounced gently when the Grand Old Duke and his men were marching. When they were up, so were the legs. When they were down, the legs were down too. Lots of exercise for the grown-ups' legs, and much open-mouthed fun for the little ones. Furthermore, for Connor and for the group of lapsitting creeper-crawlers, the Grand Old Duke marched again and again pleasurably.

From the "Itsy Bitsy Spider" to "London Bridge," many nursery rhymes have tunes and actions suited to their words. The tunes help babies to remember the rhymes, and the whole-body actions give them a chance to perform and an excuse to move around while fingerplay exercises a baby's fine- and gross-motor coordination. Good finger wiggling leads to page turning and eventually writing. And besides, they are irresistibly fun.

Books to Get Bodies Moving and Fingers Wiggling

Several books achieve the gold standard for finger plays. Because of them, you need not worry about remembering or learning the gestures. They include easy diagrams for you and fun illustrations for baby.

- *Pat-a-Cake and Other Play Rhymes,* Joanna Cole and Stephanie Calmenson, Alan Tiegreen (illus.). With hand claps, finger wiggles, and bouncing motion you'll both trot to Boston or ride a cock-horse to Banbury Cross.

- *Favorite Finger Rhymes,* Marc Tolon Brown. His diagrams for you and fun illustrations for baby make this book entertaining for you both. *Party Rhymes* offers further funny and playful song-rhymes that encourage us to sing along with "Here We Go Round the Mulberry Bush" and other favorites.

- **Piggies,** Audrey Wood, Don Wood (illus.). The Woods offer an all-new finger rhyme filled with fat, smart, long, silly, and wee little piggies all cleverly illustrated on a pair of baby hands.

- **Knock at the Door, and Other Baby Action Rhymes,** Kay Chorao. This is a wonderful collection of rhymes illustrated with small but clear boxes showing you which nose to touch, finger to tug, or direction to bend.

- **Head, Shoulders, Knees, & Toes and Other Action Rhymes,** Zita Newcome. They are all here—from toe touching, boat rowing, to baabaa-ing action fun.

- **This Little Piggy with CD : Lap Songs, Finger Plays, Clapping Games, and Pantomime Rhymes,** Jane Yolen, Adam Stemple, Will Hillenbrand (illus.). Full of fun by this famous writer mother and her musical son.

Growing Up with Fingerplay

In the beginning, moms and dads need to help their babies move their arms up and down, or swing from side to side, to the lyrics of the nursery rhyme or song. These delightful and useful baby calisthenics prepare a baby for the feeling of moving to the rhythm and introduce the repetitive motions. Two to three reps will do for now.

When the children are able to hold things in their hands and move around on their own, the finger and body actions can become more elaborate. Can they eensy-weensy their hands into a sunshine arc? Can they jump with Jack over a make-believe candlestick? Can they wiggle a finger to recognize Tall Man or Thumbkin? Yes.

Soon the big kids will hokey-pokey and really dance with you. They will march with the Grand Old Duke of York, and boogie with a rhythm from a heavily accented poem or rhyme and certainly from the music you provide.

Start Every Day with a Song

Music is vitally important. We all prick up our ears at the sound of a voice singing a familiar tune, a hum, a whistle, or even the music of water rushing into the tub. We are born with an innate appreciation for sounds and music, beats and rhythm, and that appreciation reveals itself almost from birth. Additionally, music makes a significant difference in our lives. Besides the research about how Mozart and Bach help develop the brain and our capacities to do math and science, therapists report that music helps children experience a wider and deeper range of emotions.

Try using the same song to announce a familiar, repeated activity, like a diaper change, pulling a shirt over the head, or a bath. You'll quickly start seeing signs that your baby knows what's coming next!

Like books, when music is present in a child's life it can seep into every interaction. Parents find themselves singing almost without realizing it. Babies love it whether you are in or out of tune. Doug, a brand new father of an infant daughter, found himself singing "Silent Night" to baby Azia within the first twenty-four hours of her birth. Yes, she was born around Christmas, but he said it was somewhat instinctive. "Silent Night" seemed like a lullaby as it emerged from him. Hearing it comforted both newborn baby and newborn daddy.

Why talk about music in a book about reading? Partly because so many great books bring songs to life. Music is part of a culture, and a way of learning a language. And partly because we love, need, and use it. Music appeals to us in a way other art forms don't (or can't). Fast, cheerful music takes our mood up, slower tunes bring us back down. Speech and writing have elements of music, as do illustrations that suggests rhythm and movement. Music resonates at a profound level for all of us. It nurtures something deep within. It gives us pleasure.

> *"One-year-old Eric calms down the minute we approach the CD player. As soon as he sees one of us fiddling with the buttons, he stops crying and settles down. Then when the music is on, he smiles and twirls his feet. Since we have pretty eclectic tastes he does too. He responds to everything from Elvis to Coldplay to Mozart."* —Jennifer

Every "baby class," nursery, and preschool includes music and singing. To grab the attention of one or more babies or children, all a librarian or preschool teacher needs to do is sing. "Hello, hello, hello and how do you do?" Songs get everyone involved. As anyone who's found themselves humming "Baby Beluga" alone at the grocery store would attest, some songs are irresistible. That musical assist to memory makes it easier to learn things—like the alphabet. We'll bet there's a *Schoolhouse Rock* lesson lurking in your memory somewhere. "Conjunction Junction," anyone?

A song can help make the transition from one activity to another easier (a "clean-up" song is common at many baby and toddler activities). Repeating the same song at the same time of day is soothing for a little one, and hearing the songs from home in a new environment or with a new person can be comforting, too.

Songs are also satisfying because the verses set up expectations that are then fulfilled in the refrains. Rhythmic repetitions arouse anticipation and simultaneously soothe or answer it. A song or rhyme with a satisfying finish can be repeated over and over again (think "This Little Piggy" or "Old MacDonald"). Books, new and old, work in the same way. A story begins and our interest is captured. We wonder what is coming next. Songs and books both satisfy that urge for completion—for a beginning and an end and the opportunity to do it all over again.

Featured Book
The Baby Goes Beep
Rebecca O'Connell
and
Ken Wilson-Max (illus.)

Babies sing too, or at least they sputter, crow, and blow raspberries. Here is a book that understands how much a babbling baby has to say during the day. All parents will recognize the beeping baby, and some babies will be delighted to have a character in a book who actually speaks their language.

Ask your older child to sing to your baby to distract her at a difficult moment or just help change her mood from fussy to interested. A song (freshly invented or an old favorite) is a great attention-getter, an older sibling even more so, and the two together can be golden.

Growing Up with Music Playing

Babies respond to all kinds of music. Whether the parents sing well or poorly; whether it's Bach, Mozart, and the classics or whether there's some Lena Horne or Cher in the mix, babies all respond in mood and gesture. Older babies love to move and groove to the rhythm of songs and music. You can dance with them in your arms or fly them around the room to just about any song. They'll also like watching you clap, shake a rattle, or bang a drum to the beat.

Toddlers will want a rattle or a drum of their own. It's fun to practice making a noise REALLY LOUD and then soft again and to listen to songs that allow you to move along, like "The Hokey Pokey." A child in a "music class" may refuse to shake his rattle or dance along in class but perform willingly at home. It takes time to get comfortable with new skills, and many kids like to absorb what other children are doing before they join in.

When they grow to the sing-along stage, new fun can begin. Include silly songs like the rhyming name game (Mary Mary Bo Berry, Banana Fanna Fo Ferry, Fe Fi Fo Farry, Ma-ry). Make up your own. At first, your child may laugh or protest if you begin substituting silly words for those of a favorite song. Later, he'll add his own. The more kids feel comfortable with singing, the more exuberant they will be. They'll sing out with gusto.

What Did the Doggy in the Window Look Like?
Books to Illustrate Favorite Songs

- **Oh Where, Oh Where?,** John Porter. Where, oh where, has my little bear gone? He's hiding, quite obviously, on each and every page from the gently searching big bear. Simple pastel illustrations create a comforting scene.

- **Skip to My Lou,** Mary Ann Hoberman, Nadine Bernard Westcott (illus.). Pigs in the parlor, cats in the buttermilk, and the animals are taking over the farm. The story is all there in the pictures, the words of the song are cleverly expanded, and everybody can join in the chorus.

- **Down by the Bay (Raffi Songs to Read),** Raffi, Nadine Bernard Westcott (illus.). The watermelons grow in profusion, and the children and lively characters are dancing all about, down by the bay. (You can't go wrong with any of Raffi's books. They are all playful songs and full of toddler fun.)

- **Row, Row, Row Your Boat (Board Books for Babies),** Annie Kubler. All of Annie Kubler's series of songs are adorable and immediately accessible for toddlers. (The series includes *If You're Happy and You Know It*, *Ring Around a Rosie*, and *Head, Shoulder, Knees, and Toes*. Toddlers love them all.)

- **Down by the Station,** Will Hillenbrand. This train is a zoo train, picking up baby animals on the way to the children's zoo and leaving room for an adventure or two along the way. With extra verses for each animal and even animal sounds.

- **Little Bunny Foo Foo : Told and Sung by the Good Fairy,** Paul Brett Johnson. Can a mischievous bunny get three magic wishes if he stops bopping small forest creatures on the head with mud pies? (If you prefer the variation that implies a bop with a mallet or hammer, try *Little Rabbit Foo Foo*, Michael Rosen, Arthur Robins (illus.). Both are great fun and infinitely repeatable.)

Why Can't He Just Listen to My Music?

Your first kids' CDs will probably arrive as gifts. Who is Raffi, and why would my toddler listen to an Australian boy band called the Wiggles? If you're one of the many parents who rule out specialty music because you're going to raise your kid on real music, you might want to think again. Rock-and-roll and opera have their places, and you'll want your child to enjoy, or at least listen to, your favorites—but there's something about kids' music that gets them moving and singing. There are some wonderful artists working in the children's music field today, and you may find yourself enjoying a new version of "Polly Wolly Doodle" just as much as your baby. Just like celebrities and authors, when musicians have kids they're often inspired to create something that's right for them. You'll find famous names like Dan Zanes (formerly of the Del Fuegos), Tom Paxton, and They Might Be Giants mixed in with great work by Laurie Berkner, Joe McDermott, and Daddy-A-Go-Go. Give them a try…and give Raffi and the Wiggles a chance.

Featured Book

Philadelphia Chickens!

Sandra Boynton

The book has funny pictures, lyrics, and even musical notation, and the CD features every song in an "Imaginary musical revue" starring artists like Meryl Streep and the Bacon Brothers. This book/CD combo is perfect for long car trips and sing-alongs.

Great Music to Enjoy with Your Child

- **No!,** They Might Be Giants. There really are songs on this album you might willingly listen to when your kids aren't in the car. Fans of the band might not be surprised at the turn to kids' music, since much of their adult music had a fanciful, surreal twist that works perfectly when applied to "Fibber Island" (where they meet friends from Mars and sew buttons on their hats). The title track might be the only thing that could make the word "No" funny again.

- **Victor Vito,** Laurie Berkner. Berkner will be familiar to all parents of Noggin fans as the sprightly redhead whose kid-style music videos, featuring dancing kids as well as her band in a stark white studio, appear in between episodes of *Blue's Clues* and *Franklin*. Her cheerful original songs will get the whole family moving.

- **Rocket Ship Beach,** Dan Zanes. It's no surprise that when the former front man for Del Fuego turns his attention to kids music, he'll come up with something that makes both the front and the back seats happy. This CD includes both hip versions of old standards like "Polly Wolly Doodle" and inventive new songs, as well as a reggae-rap "Father Goose" featuring dancehall rapper Rankin' Don.

- **Baby Beluga,** Raffi. Something about the name Raffi just puts off some parents. We imagine mind-numbing, new-age croonings that will leave us banging our heads against a wall. In reality, Raffi's popularity is well deserved; his songs are bright and clever and while they may appeal more to your child than to you, that is, after all, what they're for.

- **For the Kids,** Various Artists. A compilation CD created to benefit VH1's Save the Music foundation, on a mission to restore music education in public schools across the country. Offers the priceless opportunity to hear Bare Naked Ladies singing "La La La La Lemon" and Sarah McLaughlin's soulful rendition of "The Rainbow Connection," plus original songs by Bleu and Tom Waits.

Ages and Stages: Simple Suggestions

Newborn	• Play music in the nursery. Babies don't need total silence! • Sing or say whatever you remember of songs, poems, advertisements, and nursery rhymes. You'll get better at it and the baby will always love your voice.
Heads Up	• Move baby's arms or legs according to a rhyme or song you're singing. • Invent a diaper changing song. (Or several. Or several hundred.) • Play a game of Hokey-Pokey, carrying the little one on your hip and putting your right hands in, then your left legs….then shake them all about.
Sitting	• Bang on a pot festival! Open your kitchen cupboards and give the budding musician a wooden spoon. • Do the "Chicken Soup with Rice" song and dance at meal time when you've got the little one captive in her high chair.
Crawling/Creeping	• Actions that go with nursery rhymes are starting to be copied, remembered, and lots of fun.

Cruising/Walking	• Try some stand-up nursery rhymes or songs, with gestures for him to imitate.
Talking (a few words)	• Stop reading the whole rhyming sentence and let your baby add the missing word. Simple Simon met a _____, or Jack be nimble, Jack be quick, Jack jump over the _____.
Talking More	• He can probably remember his first full nursery rhyme, with some prompting. • Sing made-up songs to accompany everything you do: bath-time, kitchen cooking and clean up, walking the dog. • Act one out. You be Miss Muffett, and he can be the spider.
Running (but not talking much)	• Marching in different styles: sideways steps, giant steps, scissors steps. (See *Jonathan and His Mommy*, Irene Smalls, Michael Hays (illus.) and *Will You Carry Me?*, Heleen van Rossum, Peter van Harmelen (illus.) for joyous steps.) • Play a rhyming game of identifying ordinary things that rhyme. Bring me something that sounds like hall? Ball. Like power? Flower. Like bat? Cat.

Talking ALL THE TIME!	• Take notebooks into the park or the playground. Compose a poem about the place together.
	• Play rhyming games. Remember the old "name game" song of old? Dust it off now for maximum fun. Mary Mary Bo Berry Banana Fanna Fo Ferry Fee Fi Fo Fary…Ma-ry; Sam Sam Bo Bam, Banana Fanna Fo Fam, Fee Fi Fo Fam, Sa-am.
	• Cut sandwiches with cookie cutters, making stars, gingerbread guys, candy canes, or children, then sing or tell stories featuring these characters. We call them peanut-butter-persons. Then eat.

Chapter Eight:
Books and the Big Boxes: TV, Computers, and Your Baby Reader

TV is a fact of life. Like the rest of their families, most babies, toddlers, and preschoolers in this country watch some television—and they enjoy it. And many parents struggle with that fact. We agonize over the amount of TV our kids watch, the programs, and the effects. We judge ourselves by it and we judge others. As a result, sometimes, when we're feeling pressure to come across as the super mom or the great dad, we…lie. We downplay the amount of time involved; we excuse the enthusiastic bellowing of the catchy *Bob the Builder* song as the result of too much time with a neighbor child. In fact, we deny the enthusiasm our children bring to this supposedly low-brow activity.

Stop making yourself crazy. For one thing, when you turn TV into a forbidden pleasure you make it more appealing, and your children will pick up on your attitude. For another, when you embrace good children's programming you support it and encourage the development of more of the same. Finally, and perhaps most importantly, parents should support each other (and ourselves) in every aspect of the tough job we do. No one is going to die if to you plop the kid down in front of Noggin to take a breather.

Don't make a big deal out of choosing some "baby TV" when kids are sharing the TV. If you don't announce that your older kid won't like it, she may surprise you. *Sesame Street* is great for mixed ages, but plenty of "big kids" enjoy *Teletubbies* and baby videos, especially if they're old favorites.

Of course, the media debate will continue, and every time it's possible to grab your attention by announcing that watching TV causes ADD, obesity, or a delay in learning, you're going to see it, ironically enough, on the TV news. Obviously, flickering, stimulating, noisy adult television is unintelligible to a baby and incomprehensible for a toddler. But most of the negative studies of children and television do not distinguish between adult programming and shows designed for kids. In fact, there's some wonderful children's television out there. At its best, it's educational. Children who watch *Blue's Clues* regularly score higher on cognitive tests. At the very least, in moderation, it's harmless. Let's acknowledge that some TV is often a part of the day, and declare that in a life otherwise filled with books and playtime and music, there's absolutely nothing wrong with that.

Why Talk about TV in a Book on Reading?

It may come as something of a surprise that in a book focused on reading we're not going to condemn TV (or computers) as inherently evil. Good television programming can combine sight and sound to create a unique learning experience. Some computer games are great learning tools, too. We're certainly not advocating two-year-olds slumped in front of either box for hours a day, eyes glazed and mind on autopilot, but kids can learn from good shows and good programs.

So, why talk about TV in a book about reading? Partly because it's impossible to avoid—so many books are based on TV shows and TV shows are based on books. Partly because there's a growing concern that TV and reading are mutually exclusive—that kids raised with the box will never crack open a book. That doesn't have to be the case. This chapter is designed to help you find ways to use TV to encourage and enrich reading and playtime instead of taking their place.

TV and videos getting a little out of hand at your house? Use a vacation or having visitors to interrupt regular viewing habits. Then reintroduce TV time back in gradually at a level you're more comfortable with.

If you're a no-television household, then TV and videos aren't going to be an issue for you (although you may be surprised by your kids' interest in the TV tie-in books at the book store). You may choose not to expose such young children to computers, either. But for most of us, screen time of one sort or another (and the two are growing ever closer) is part of our culture. The big boxes aren't going away anytime soon. Now is a good time to begin figuring out what role these increasingly dominant media will play in your child's life.

Book-Friendly, Kid-Friendly TV and Videos

It's no exaggeration to say that TV is pop culture. It's a fact of life. A first-grader with absolutely no awareness of *SpongeBob SquarePants* is going to be somewhat out of place in most American communities. At some point, kids are going to want to watch what's popular. That's clearly not true of babies, and not for most toddlers or preschoolers, either.

Even kids in day care or preschool aren't really aware that their friends may do or watch something different than they do at home. One child may know all the words to the *Bob the Builder* theme song and another may not, but three minutes of listening to a friend bellow it out will fix that. What's more, they don't see any distinction between "Can We Fix It?" and "Jingle Bells." They're just having fun.

So there's probably no pressure on you to let a young child watch anything in particular, or indeed, anything at all. You can pick and choose the programming that works for you and your child. And whatever you choose, you can ensure that it's part of a day filled with reading and other activities…because at this point, they can't work the remote!

The "Video Board Book" for Babies

What is there for a baby under three to watch? For newborns, nothing. The truth is, their eyes just aren't set up yet to take in anything on television, although they might enjoy the music. It isn't until five or six months that they begin to have the depth perception and focusing ability necessary to view an object on the screen.

There are plenty of videos designed for slightly older babies. Most present screen shots of simple objects and toys, rotating or rolling or doing whatever they do, with a background of classical music, children's music, or even identification of the object in several languages. Some wash the screen with a color, then say the color name, or offer and identify a shape. Some show puppets interacting with babies to identify, describe, and sort the objects. All are intentionally slow and free of confusing narrative or flash editing.

Julie Clark, founder of the Baby Einstein Company (now owned by Disney), created the first of these "baby videos." She likened her products to "video board books."

Assuming there's an adult watching with the baby to identify the things on the screen, the comparison is not entirely incorrect, but the tactile experience of a book is missing. Though the "educational value," at least with respect to the object, is the same (or even enhanced by the addition of sound), there's nothing to chew, no pages to turn, and no underlying lesson about the joys of a book. The baby can't control it or interact with it. From that point of view, the video board book is a poor shadow of the real thing.

"Video Board Books" for Babies

Baby Einstein: *Baby Mozart: Music Festival, Baby Bach: Musical Adventure.* There are many titles in this series, but we like the originals, created by Julie Aigner-Clark before the sale to Disney.

Fisher Price: *Baby's Day, Musical Baby, Baby Moves, Nature Baby.*

Baby Nick Jr.: *Curious Buddy Series.* With titles like Curious Buddies: Look and Listen at the Park and Exploring at the Beach

Brainy Baby: *Left Brain, Right Brain.* These take the educational premise a bit far by introducing French, Spanish and early math concepts, but there are plenty of baby faces and toys to engage your baby.

Mommy and Me Playgroup Favorites: *Splish Splash.*

PBS Kids: *Teletubbies.* People either love or hate this oddly mesmerizing show with its baby-talking life-sized puppet creatures frolicking through their evergreen land and offering a very early introduction to concepts like color and shape and basic social lessons.

But you can't read board books, or any books, to your baby all the time. Nor can you play peek-a-boo, dance, and sing for all of baby's waking hours. For those times when she's not willing to sit on the floor and explore a pile of books or toys and you aren't feeling up to performing, the "video board book" might be just perfect. Watch it with her some of the time. Talk about what you see. But just as you let her play with books on her own sometimes, there's no harm in letting her watch on her own while you shower, read, or work. Try to banish the "electronic baby-sitter" guilt.

Toddler TV

Gone are the days when the only educational television came out of the Children's Television Workshop and most other viewing involved falling anvils or hunting "wabbits." Twenty-odd years ago, Susan's son Ben had memorized the video they'd made of a *Charlie Brown* special and could recite it, complete with character voice imitations. His sister Emma was conquering her fear of the Wicked Witch of the West at two, and, as "Dorfy," traveled regularly to her own imaginary Oz, stuffed dog Toto and basket in hand. Today there are more programs than ever before, and even a whole cable network (Noggin) directed specifically at toddlers. Noggin's slogan ("It's like preschool on TV!") may be somewhat cringe-inducing (we think you need teachers, other children, scissors, paper, books, paints, snacks, and above all, interaction, before you achieve preschool status). But its programming, like the toddler and preschool offerings on PBS Kids, the Disney Channel's Playhouse Disney and Nickelodeon's Nick Jr., is perfect for its young audience. Every show is simple and offers take-away lessons that you can use in a package your child will enjoy.

What About the Commercials?

Here's the thing about commercials aimed at babies and toddlers—they work. Justine was changing channels, looking for a program for three-year-old Hailey, when she paused at a Dannon commercial. As the familiar logo filled the screen, Hailey turned to her mother and said, "I want yogurt."

So if you want your child to develop a pressing need for anything and everything that advertisers choose to put in front of her, then commercials are fine. If not, you might want to avoid them. As of this writing, Noggin and PBS Kids have no commercials, but allow sponsors for their shows to include a short, non-product oriented message with their name and logo. In other words, if your child is familiar with McDonald's, it will make him think about McDonald's, and if not, it won't. The Disney Channel is, in a sense, commercial free, although it's hard to avoid the fact that Disney is itself a product. Nickelodeon and the broadcast networks show commercials in between, but not during, the shows, which means that a vigilant parent with a remote, DVR, or VCR can avoid them completely. Most videos or DVDs include commercials for other videos or even movies, but these are easily skipped as long as you're in charge of the machinery.

These shows are not designed for you. If you watch too long, you may feel your brain leeching out of your eyeballs. There are no inside jokes and no clever references—nothing in fact, to take the toddler away from the story. That's what makes them work so well for small children.

Of course, there's a catch. Kids have been watching television since it first flickered its way into our lives and living rooms, but a primary difference between the way we watched then and the way we watch now is that families used to all watch same thing together. Twenty-five years ago *The Wizard of Oz* was an annual TV event, not a DVD, and kids enjoyed it curled up on the sofa between Mom and Dad. There may be more programming out there for toddlers, and toddlers may be able to get more out of it than ever before, but if you're going to refer back to the time Cyril wet his pants or the lessons learned in today's episode, you're going to have to watch too.

We understand that you're not encouraging your child to watch TV because you have a pressing desire to see the animated version of Maisy. That's fine. Here's our suggestion—watch with her at least once. Try to stay nearby, so that you can field questions, reinforce any lessons, and just generally know what's going on. As with books, your child learns better if you're with her. She needs you to take anything away from these programs, but once you're on board, she'll gain by watching alone as well. For her, repetition is key to understanding. You're going to have the hang of Miffy's Same Game (and know its catchy little song) after one viewing.

Eleven Great Programs (Video, DVD, or Live) for Toddlers and Twos

1. **Miffy.** With animation that's scarcely more active than the pages of the books themselves and a narrated voiceover, Miffy tells simple stories about Miffy's life, interspersed with simple math games you can adapt for use at home. One of the few shows with an educational component that goes beyond moral lessons about friendship.

2. **Maisy.** The straightforward, matter-of-fact voice of the narrator actually addresses Maisy and her friends as they encounter common toddler problems, like forgetting to go to the bathroom, and fantasies, like driving a train or a plane.

3. *Kipper.* Kipper's simple adventures take place against a very plain background, with just the relevant details included, which makes them easy for kids to focus on. Also nice because the lessons on friendship (the only lessons even arguably included) are subtle, never preachy.

4. *Bob the Builder.* These talking construction vehicles entrance most children. Although clearly a sidekick, Wendy appears to be Bob's equal in the construction business, a nice gender-neutral touch, and the townspeople come in all races, shapes, and sizes—rare in cartoons and claymation, which generally handle diversity by creating blue and green and purple people rather than using more prevalent skin tones. Bob and Wendy hammer home the moral a little too hard at times, but kids don't seem to notice.

5. *Blue's Clues.* This program (Blue the puppy leaves three clues to help viewers solve a simple riddle in each episode) genuinely teaches children useful reasoning skills and problem solving with every episode, and yet it's completely entertaining to them. They don't tune out or become suspicious when the learning starts, because it's all part and parcel of the whole. Takes the political correctness thing a little far by celebrating "Love Day" and "Thankfulness Day" instead of Valentine's Day and Thanksgiving, but it's tough to fault anyone for being too inclusive.

6. *Sesame Street/Elmo's Room.* This is the classic, the one kids' program almost everyone is happy to see. Because it's something of a variety show and not very predictable (each season did different things in a different order, and all seasons are rerun constantly, so that there's no consistent format), some toddlers won't be able to enjoy it until they're a little older. If yours doesn't want to stay tuned, save the whole program for later and try an Elmo video or DVD instead.

7. *Caillou.* This is perhaps the most realistic children's program available, about a sometimes whiny four-year-old doing everyday four-year-old things, like getting sick, learning to ice skate, and struggling to deal with his younger sister. It's an idealized life but one with plenty of useful lessons and encouragement for kids having the same experiences.

8. *Oswald.* This surreal, colorful little program about an octopus and his friends, a penguin and a flower, holds younger children's attention just through the artwork and animation and offers funny stories and unusually presented lessons for older toddlers and up. ("Try new things" is conveyed by a day in which the more adventurous Oswald has all kinds of good things happen to him, while "just like always" Henry the penguin misses out.)

9. *Jack's Big Music Show.* Puppet Jack and his friends dance and play in a music-filled clubhouse, but the real attraction is the kid-music videos from Laurie Berkner and other artists, all perfect for a little living room dance party.

10. *Clifford.* Clifford and friends teach those ubiquitous lessons about feelings and friendship but with a nice pro-reading message in every episode.

11. *Tiny Planets.* This unusual program offers early science and physics education (how high do things bounce, how can you build stronger structures) in the form of visits to different planets. Aliens Bing and Bong help odd, inarticulate creatures with even odder dilemmas at each stop. The computer generated artistry is detailed, witty, and impressive.

Where Do the Books Come in? (Enter the Marketing Team, Stage Left)

Sesame Street, *Blue's Clues* and *Dora the Explorer* all have at least two things in common. They're clever, honestly educational programs created especially for toddlers and preschoolers. And they have toy and book and clothing tie-ins galore. Shows like *Maisy*, *Max and Ruby*, and *Clifford* come from the other side of the spectrum: they were books first, television second. Either way, if one of these programs becomes your child's favorite, you'll find plenty to delight her on the bookstore shelves.

Books That Started It All: Great Books That Became Good Television

- **Clifford the Big Red Dog,** Norman Bridwell.
- **Rolie Polie Olie,** William Joyce.
- **Bunny Cakes** (Max and Ruby), Rosemary Wells.
- **I Will Never Not Ever Eat a Tomato** (Charlie and Lola), Lauren Child.
- **Maisy Goes to Bed,** Lucy Cousins.
- **Miffy,** Dick Bruna.
- **Winnie the Pooh,** A. A. Milne.
- **Thomas the Tank Engine,** Wilbert Awdry, C. Reginald Dalby (illus.).
- **Little Bear,** Else Holmelund Minarik, Maurice Sendak (illus.).
- **Miss Spider,** David Kirk.

You'll have to make your own decision about whether your child's wardrobe should reflect her television passion, but when it comes to the associated books and toys, we do see some real advantages. Here's one area where the old-fashioned technology of a book is actually an improvement over the video: you can take it with you. It's a physical companion, a little bit of your child's video friends that can come along in the stroller or car seat. Your child can freeze the action as long as she wants and return to certain pages or moments in the story again and again without the help of an adult with a remote control. Generally, books that were books first and television shows second read better than books that were created as TV tie-ins, but either way, they really work.

Books and toys encourage kids to take the characters they've already fallen in love with beyond the screen. If Blue can go for her check-up in the book, she can go for her check-up on your couch, too, and maybe Mommy and the rest of your toys can be patients as well. She doesn't always sound like the Blue on TV, and she doesn't always do things in the exact same order. It's liberating. There's a great fear that watching videos (or television) of favorite characters will replace children's ability to imagine characters of their own. It may be that a child who's seen a moving, talking video character may be fascinated enough to add that character to their play repertoire, but for most kids, what they've seen isn't going to be enough. They're going to want to bring the character into their world.

For toddlers, the appeal of these books is also the extension of the familiar. These characters are proven through years of strong kid appeal (or heavily test-marketed and designed to appeal to your child)—which is why you'll find kids who've never watched a program gravitating towards the tie-in shelves. If the effect of all this market research spooks you, remember that the *Sesame Street* characters were designed in the same way. It's not necessarily done with wholly commercial intentions.

"Sam certainly watches some kids' television, but even the shows that bring some of his favorite characters to life don't seem to have affected the way he sees them. The Percy on the Thomas the Tank Engine *videos may be a boy, but the Percy on his train table is a girl, and his Thomas can fly. Occasionally his Thomas acts out something from a video, but for the most part, he leads his own odd little life. The day I overheard Thomas learning to be a sushi chef, I stopped worrying about Sam's imagination for good." —KJ*

Books associated with television programs or videos can also help ease your child's transition from board books to longer stories with more narrative. They can encourage a child to sit alone and turn the pages—another step on the road to reading. For older children, the increased familiarity with the characters and illustrations makes them prime learn-to-read material. There's something about being comfortable with the story structure and the pictures that makes it easier to take a risk like trying to read the words.

And most importantly, a book is a book, whether it evolved into television or was based on a television character. It's a subliminal reminder that entertainment is not confined to the big box. Reading may link your child to a program or video he knows and loves, but it engages him in a different way.

TALKING TO THE AUTHOR   NORMAN BRIDWELL

What's it like to have your book turned into a TV show? Norman Bridwell, writer and creator of Clifford, knows.

I was really delighted because I knew it would be a quality product if Scholastic was producing it and PBS was going to show it. Somebody else was interested in doing a Clifford show years ago, and they wanted gangs of boys, they wanted conflict, they wanted evil villains. And that's just not Clifford. Clifford is a gentle, nurturing character, and I think PBS is the right spot for him. There aren't any disasters or car chases. It's a nice, gentle show. I've watched my six-year-old granddaughter sit absolutely glued to the set. She's a very active little girl, but during *Clifford* she sits. It's almost like *Mr. Rogers* with fur.

Is Educational TV Really Educational?

Do kids learn from TV? Absolutely. Researchers have found that babies as young as twelve months can take a cue from a video of a woman reacting negatively to an enticing object. When offered a choice between that object and another, babies avoid the item they've seen create the negative affect. Will an hour of *Sesame Street* "sponsored by the letter A" help a toddler recognize the letter A? Yes, especially (always the catch) if the lesson is reinforced by a living person.

> **Stick to age-appropriate programs for as long as you can. It's worth noting that *Blue's Clues* is intended for ages three to six, and often features reading or pre-reading activities, yet some parents consider their four- and five-year olds to have "grown out of it." Be honest: which of you is really tired of *Sesame Street*?**

From age two on, high-quality programs can actually increase vocabulary, letter-sound knowledge, comprehension, and the ability to follow and relate to a narrative. It appears that kids can and do learn from programs like *Blue's Clues* that are designed to teach and achieve educational goals in each episode. Colors and shapes appear and are described, words are written on the screen, snacks are measured and counted, and your child learns.

True literacy is reading, writing, speaking, and listening. For children three and under, the last two are primary. TV and videos provide content for them—fodder for their own conversations. Watching improves listening skills and gives them something to talk about. Of course, they may learn a few other things, too. The creators of kids' TV excel when it comes to teaching letters, colors, and other concepts. Things get a little fuzzier when it comes to behavior. There's no guarantee that your child will remember the moral of a story instead of imitating the bad behavior that led up to it. "Mean words hurt" may not cancel out the clarion call of "Stupid!"

The key, again, is to know what shows and videos your child is watching. This allows you to reinforce the positive lesson, especially if some of the less desirable behaviors start showing up in your child. It also allows you to reinforce any new vocabulary as well as narrative skills by encouraging your child to tell you about what she watched. Sometimes, if you want TV to be specifically educational, you're going to have to dig in and create the education yourself.

> *"Joey loves every detail of the ever-popular Thomas videos, and he's definitely learning from them. "'Out of my way," Gordon said as he rushed past,' he'll shout as he runs through the room. Only three, but his ability to write fictional dialogue already seems secure." —Laura*

Audio Books for Babies and Toddlers (A Treat for Them, a Break for You!)

Many parents swear by audio books. Audio books can work for babies as a soothing pre-nap listen or background noise in the car. A pleasant voice and rhythmic words please almost any baby, and the more familiar a particular tape (or CD) becomes, the happier it will make her. Toddlers can hold a book themselves and learn to turn the pages at the "ding" sound—another great activity for the back of the car or rest-time.

{ *New mom Amanda, on leave from her job in publishing, remembers being stunned by the amount of time she spent sidelined, nursing her newborn. She couldn't juggle a book, daytime TV left her cold, and she was desperate for some distraction. Her office sent over audio books of all the Newberry award winners (some of the best books for older children). Her baby boy seemed to find them just as soothing as she did.* }

Longer audio books, without an accompanying picture book, might please toddlers in the car as well, and they definitely work for an older child with a toddler sibling. Most bookstores carry audio/picture book sets, and libraries have a large selection to borrow. For longer audio books, you may have to check online bookstores, catalogs (Chinaberry usually has a nice selection), or order from your local bookstore. Many are also available for download at Audible.com.

Twelve Great Listens

Most audio books can be listened to in snippets online. It's a great help to all of us. And don't forget Audible.com if you use any kind of MP3 player.

1. ***Abiyoyo,*** Pete Seeger, Michael Hays (illus.). Book and CD. Famous book with Seeger singing and telling it himself and a wonderful story to hear repeatedly.

2. ***Alexander and the Terrible, Horrible, No Good, Very Bad Day, and Other Stories and Poems,*** Judith Viorst. Alexander's rotten day is the perfect lead-off for this humorous collection of Judith Viorst's stories and poems about the ups and downs of childhood, read by Blythe Danner. Also included are: *Alexander, Who Used to Be Rich Last Sunday* and *The Tenth Good Thing About Barney.*

3. ***Green Eggs and Ham and Other Servings of Dr. Seuss,*** Dr. Seuss. Nine complete stories read by the likes of Jason Alexander and David Hyde Pierce.

4. ***Mouse Tales** and **Mouse Soup,*** Arnold Lobel (author and reader). "Papa, please tell us a tale." When Papa's seven little mouse boys ask for a bedtime story, Papa does even better than that—he tells seven stories, one for each boy! *Mouse Soup* finds Mouse in a jam—soon he'll be weasel soup! Just in time, he thinks up a clever and entertaining way to distract weasel from serving up mouse soup for supper.

5. ***The Cat in the Hat and Other Dr. Seuss Favorites,*** Dr. Seuss. Nine more complete stories, read by luminaries like Kelsey Grammer, Dustin Hoffman, and John Cleese.

6. ***Animals Should Definitely Not Wear Clothing,*** Judi Barrett. Read along…because a snake would lose it, a billy goat would eat it for lunch, and it would always be wet on a walrus! This well-loved book by Judi and Ron Barrett shows the very youngest why animals' clothing is perfect…just as it is.

7. **Corduroy,** Don Freeman. Available in English or Spanish. This little girl and her chosen bear remain enchanting and endearing. (Also *A Pocket for Corduroy*.)

8. **Joseph Had a Little Overcoat,** Simms Taback. In today's throwaway world, Joseph's old-fashioned frugality is a welcome change. Based on a Yiddish song from Simms Taback's youth (lyrics and music reproduced on the last page), the book is filled with delightful rhythms and arresting colors.

9. **Jump, Frog, Jump!,** Robert Kalan, Byron Barton (illus.) Here's a simple cumulative tale about what happens when a frog wants to eat a fly.

10. **Mama Don't Allow,** Thacher Hurd. Wonderful for its jazzy music and bayou feel, this is a story of a band playing their hearts out at the alligator ball...until they discover that they're on the menu for the final feast.

11. **Snowy Day,** Ezra Jack Keats, Linda Terheyden (narrator). A favorite story of a child's first snowfall read aloud

12. **I Lost My Bear,** Jules Feiffer. A theatrical reading of Jules Feiffer's story about a young girl's anguished search for her favorite bear.

TV that Gives Bookpower a Boost

Toddlers and preschoolers often develop an all-consuming interest in a particular subject. They can be surprisingly sophisticated about the information that interests them—if it involves their beloved trucks, snakes, or planets, they'll remember it. You can foster that interest with books and videos. Discovery-style "why" books, like the *Magic School Bus* or the *I Wonder Why* series, are usually designed for older kids, but you can look at the pictures together and edit the text appropriately, and learn something new with each reading.

Fortunately, you can find videos designed for young children on a variety of non-fiction subjects, as well as videos that work for all ages. These can also be a nice way for a child to share an interest with an adult. Like Sam, KJ's father loves trains, and the two are happy to watch videos on the Age of Steam together. There are videos about trucks, airplanes and airports, space travel, bugs, and every kind of animal you can imagine. Even older babies are often intrigued by animal programming. There's something about watching those other creatures, so like us and yet so different, move across the screen that excites a real interest. These nonfiction videos can often be overlooked, especially since traditional children's videos are promoted so heavily.

Put together a few packages that combine a new book, a video or DVD, and a small toy or treat (like stickers or small plastic animals) on something that interests your child to pull out on a rainy day.

Learning More from Book and Video Teams

- *National Geographic's Really Wild Animals: Deep Sea Dive* with *My Visit to the Aquarium,* Aliki; and *Hello, Fish! Visiting the Coral Reef,* Sylvia Earle.

- *Real Wheels Truck Adventures (There Goes a Fire Truck, There Goes a Garbage Truck)* with *I Stink,* Kate McMullan, Jim McMullan (illus.) and *The Little Fire Engine,* Lois Lenski.

- *The Alphabet Train* with *Big Book of Trains,* Christine Heap.

> When Matt's daughter Hailey was two, he was searching for something to interest her on a hotel TV and came across what looked like a nature program about snakes. He drew her attention to it—just as the man holding the snake popped the snake into his mouth and bit its head off. Matt finally calmed Hailey down, but over a year later, he's never been able to explain why to her satisfaction.

From "Again! Again!" to "Turn It Off!"

Parents of toddlers might fear that the "addictive" quality of TV will mean their child will "zone out" and watch anything. Instead, it turns out that those elements that make it compelling for us are exactly the same elements that turn off a toddler. We get hooked by a developing plot and stay tuned when characters are excited and all talk at once. We can tolerate some confusion; in fact, we're intrigued by it. Toddlers can't do this. It seems they get enough confusion from life itself. When it comes to television, they only want to watch what they understand and enjoy.

Most toddlers are ready to tune out when the television show is clearly not for them. But when they do understand, they want to understand even more. They want to see it again. Repetition, in videos as in books, increases a child's understanding of what's happening and allows a child to move on to anticipating what's going to happen. Anticipation leads to the ability to predict what will come next, which can give a very young child a real sense of control and mastery.

Don't put a TV or video player in your child's room. If you'd like her to be able to watch her TV while you watch yours, try a portable DVD player instead. They're increasingly inexpensive, versatile, and far easier to control.

So they want to watch their special programs again and again. Your programs, though, they don't want to watch at all. But that's difficult if the adult in the room finds the television absorbing. Nothing creates conflict like an adult who wants to watch something on TV and a child who wants the adult to watch, well, her. As anyone who has ever watched an NBA final basketball game with an articulate two-year-old can testify, it just doesn't work. "What that?" "Where it go?" "Why you say 'Oh!'?" "Why he do that?" "Why you say 'No!'?" "Why?" "Why?" "WHY?" They go quickly from trying to join you, to trying to get you to join them, to the kinds of crashes and "accidents" that always command your attention. It's not a happy picture.

Should you turn it off? Your choice. You are the adult, and you deserve the kind of break in your day that a favorite show or sporting event represents. Understanding that the baby feels she is competing for your attention may help, if it's a problem. You could offer a special snack or set out special toys for her during your TV time. You might want to encourage her to play nearby, although not right in front of the TV. Eventually she'll understand that you'll return your attention to her soon and enjoy the time for solo play.

> *"I remember watching the Wimbledon tennis tournament on TV when Ben was about twenty months old. The TV was on a shelf above his head, and he stood squarely in front of it, looking up, and declaring, 'I HATE Wimbledon!'"* —Susan

Babies, Toddlers, and Computers

Televisions are no longer the only fascinating big box in the house. Your baby and toddler watch you sitting down in front of the computer every day, and they're likely to want to join you. Plenty of toymakers, marketers, and even publishing companies are ready to help them jump on the bandwagon. There's some fun to be had with these products, but they're not likely to make you and your baby set aside your books for any length of time.

> *"Our kids love the computer. We like boohbah.com. Both my two- and three-year old (and thirty-two-year-old me!) get such a kick out of this fun, wordless site, and both kids are great at using the mouse (in our case touch-pad) because of it. It has games, art/color pages, and music pages. I do try to stop while we're still having fun. It's easy to get frustrated or fight over who gets to do what. Once that starts, we stop. We also use the computer to practice recognizing letters. They love touching the buttons so we play Touch the A. I call the letters and they find them and strike them and they go up on the screen in lowercase. I make the font extra big and the kids really love it."* —Jane

Special computer keyboards and software can allow your child to sit down, press a red key, and watch a red circle appear on the screen. It's fun, and it does convey the connection between the keyboard and the screen. Other than that, computer software generally offers the same "lessons" in colors, shapes, and letter recognition that are available in board books, and for a child under three, they require special hardware. It's expensive, and there's no evidence that starting your child off on the computer before three is going to increase her abilities later, although for children three and over, computer time seems to increase school readiness.

The interactivity of the computer is both its appeal and its downfall for children under three. Even with a special keyboard, they're likely to need your help and not just to get them set up. A missed mouse move sends them off to the parents' instructions or freezes the action. A bump to a child's keyboard placed over a regular keyboard moves it and changes the meaning of every key hit. When you're just developing fine motor control, just pushing the button you meant to push can be a challenge, and a keyboard is a ready source of frustration.

Many popular kids' websites have activities that kids under three can enjoy with an adult, no additional hardware needed. Some have short video stories with a "button" to push to reach the next "page" or a game that allows her to dress a favorite character. You may have to do the keyboard and mouse manipulation, but your child can make the decisions. These games can be a nice treat for a child who's played at your side while you pay the bills or email friends, and can gradually encourage a child to try a little mouse-work herself.

Websites That Work for Babies, Toddlers, and Twos

Keep in mind that most sites are geared towards a wide age range. Each site identified here has several activities that work for very young children, but you'll want to take a quick look and choose something you think your child can manage and enjoy before logging on with her.

- **PBSKids.org.** Games, activities, and print-out coloring pages from PBS favorites like *Teletubbies* and *Calliou*. Try Dress Caillou and Find Gilbert (Caillou's cat).

- **Nickjr.com.** Lots of games for Nick-created shows like *Max and Ruby, Blue's Clues,* and *Oswald,* plus "stories" that are read aloud using an arrow click to turn the page. Also comes with lots of built-in, flashy ads for other Nick shows, some not age-appropriate.

- **Noggin.com.** Some wonderfully slow-paced and simple games, like Miffy's Who Has More and Maisy's Letter Blocks, as well as printable activities for most shows. (Plenty of ads, too, but at least they're for age-appropriate programs.)

- **Funwithspot.com.** Simple games and printables with Eric Hill's popular little dog.

- **Tinyplanets.com.** Lots of activities, many too difficult, but a few (look for Find Bing and Match the Flockers) that young kids will enjoy.

- **Sesameworkshop.org.** Simple, non-flashy site with lots of games. Not surprisingly, those featuring Elmo work well for toddlers and twos, but check out other favorites as well.

- **HITEntertainment.com.** Activities from favorite videos like *Bob the Builder* and *Thomas the Tank Engine.*

Ages and Stages:
Making the Big Boxes Interactive

We know, you're not always watching with her. But when you are, make it fun! And here are a few simple computer activities to try.

Newborn	• Best TV strategy for the teeny-tiny? None. You and the other faces in your house are better than anything else. • If you have digital cable, try using the digital music option to provide soothing classical background music. • Moms might be able to email with one hand while nursing on the other. A happy, connected mother makes for a happier baby!
Heads Up	• If you have any baby videos, watch together, and briefly. Try to gauge whether she's able to see the things on the screen. • Giving her a disconnected mouse to hold might let you pay just one more bill with her on your lap.
Sitting	• If you're watching a baby video, gather a few things in the house that appear on the screen. Give her a ball when the ball bounces by.
Crawling/Creeping	• Let the baby video be background if she chooses. Make sure she has other things to amuse her when one is on (including books!). • Give her an old, disconnected keyboard to crawl to and bang.

Cruising/Walking	• Help her "dance" to a video with music and dancing, since she's unlikely to be able to sit still and watch anything. • With her in your lap, set a word processing program to a really large font. Let her hit the keyboard and watch the letters appear.
Talking (a few words)	• Start watching some programs with narrative together. Try to choose one and watch it over and over, then move on to another episode. Find books with a similar theme, or even a tie-in book about the episode. • Find (or draw) an image that supports one of her words. Show her the picture on the screen, then print it for her.
Talking More	• Encourage her to make up stories of her own about favorite characters. • Cut Elmo, or whoever, off of a video or cereal box and tape a straw to his back to make a puppet. Take him along on an adventure. • Check out (on your own) a website with games featuring favorite characters. Choose one you can do together and let her tell you how to move the mouse or what to click.

Running (but not talking much)	• More dancing to videos, this time with less help from you. Look for characters that appear in books, too, but moving and doing more active things that she can join in.
	• Check out (on your own) a website with games featuring favorite characters. Choose one that allows her to point to things in answer to your questions.
Talking ALL THE TIME!	• Ask her to tell you the story of the video she just watched.
	• Encourage her to make up her own story about the characters.
	• Help her to write a letter to a favorite character.
	• Start to support the lessons in the programs. If A is the letter of the day, carry it forward. If Blue makes an alphabet train, make a few letter cars yourself.
	• Can she begin to learn to use the mouse? Find a simple game on a kids' website and sit with her while she moves and clicks.

Chapter Nine:
Love, Loss, and Laughter: Books That Describe the Feelings of Life

Babies are born fully equipped with the capacity to feel. From the very beginning, they are able to interact with their new world. Every new experience brings a rush of new and intense emotions. As they grow, they learn to identify and handle their feelings—and they learn it from you.

Some babies may start with a proclivity towards being calm or active, sensitive or sturdy, needy or competent, but all operate on a constantly fluctuating emotional continuum. Every experience, whether it's a diaper change, a first taste of banana, a sniff from the family dog, or visiting Grandma, is charged with a variety of feelings.

New parents are also experiencing a rush of new and intense emotions, interrupted sleep, new anxieties, and the sudden onset of enormous responsibility. As a new parent, you must constantly consider your baby's needs and work his existence into yours, all while trying to maintain your normal sense of self. In the midst of all of this, some parents are better than others at helping a young child begin to understand and express his own feelings, but even the most empathetic parent can use a little help.

The Emotional World of Picture Books

Nowhere else is there so much potential for both baby and parent to learn something together for pleasure and profit than in the emotional world of picture books. These books offer both entertainment and comfort. Nearly every picture book has an emotional element, but many spotlight the emotions that babies and toddlers feel so intensely.

When "Again! Again!" becomes a constant refrain, you have a rare opportunity to understand something of the child's mind at work. There's often a reason behind the request. It could be pure enjoyment, or it could be that the child himself is trying to master what is happening in the book. Like Susan's Ben, who loved Ferdinand's mother's willingness to just let him be, and KJ's Sam, who used Supercat to ask for a nightlight, children use books as a way to talk about something important. No two-year-old is mature enough to say, "Mama, I feel that you are infringing on my developing personality. Please let me be who I am." Or even, "I've slept in the dark for two years but all of a sudden it's bothering me.

Featured Book

How Are You Peeling? Food with Moods

Saxton Freymann and Joost Elffers

These two author-artists have identified personalities and feelings in peppers and oranges. They invest fruits and vegetables with a delightful humanity by the deft insertion of black-eyed peas and specifically articulated eyebrow carvings. We see and understand what the lemon is feeling. Beyond its surefire entertainment value, the point of this creative and humorous book is to help us all talk about feelings that can emerge when we are in or out of groups, loved or shunned, afraid or adored.

Could I have a nightlight please?" A book raises the issue in a way the child can't. What is your child asking you to read again and again?

Feelings enliven our lives. Without love, anger, fear, joy, and excitement, what is there? Life is full of frustrations, jealousies, and disappointments, feelings of anger and sadness about loss. No child can grow up without them. So one way or another, all books for children deal with emotions. They help them look at, think about, and talk about feelings.

What Is a Feeling?

- *Feelings,* Aliki. All kinds of facial expressions suggest the feelings of the children.

- *Sometimes I Like to Curl up in a Ball,* Vicki Churchill and Charles Fuge. A young wombat chronicles a day in his life and expresses himself quite well.

- *Oh What A Busy Day!,* Gyo Fujikawa. All of her books are wonderful, and this one reveals the feelings reflected in kids' faces as they eat and play.

- *Mama, If You Had a Wish,* Jeanne Modesitt, Robin Spowart (illus.). A mommy bunny shows her unconditional love for her baby bunny—tears, fears, and all.

- *My Many Colored Days Board Book,* Dr Seuss. So many feelings and moods in such a small volume. Brilliant.

- *Sometimes I'm Bombaloo,* Rachel Vail. A really good big sister gets really angry when her baby brother messes with her things.

- ***Mrs. Biddlebox,*** Linda Smith, Marla Frazee (illus.). A grown-up lady gets up on the wrong side of bed and deals with it creatively by cooking away a very bad day. Whirling artwork supports this lady's can-do attitude.

- ***My Somebody Special,*** Sarah Weeks, Ashley Wolff (illus.). Being the last child picked up from day care is full of worries, reflected in the emotional tone of the art and the young ones' faces.

- ***Miffy Is Crying,*** Dick Bruna. As with all Bruna's Miffy books, the focus is unmistakable and clear. Miffy's tears on the cover are from losing her beloved stuffed bear.

- ***Buzzy's Big Bedtime Book,*** Harriet Ziefert, Emily Bolam (illus.). Bathtubs and bedtimes are often anxiety producing for small ones. Trust Harriet Ziefert to create short, toddler-friendly stories about these worries.

- ***The Pigeon Has Feelings, Too,*** Mo Willems. Willems's sparsely drawn pigeon reacts with characteristic testiness when the bus driver tries to command a happy face in this original board book.

What's Going On in There?

All feelings are legitimate. Some emotions are just bigger, scarier, and tougher to deal with than others. Children feel these feelings too. They come up at major times in our lives—the birth of a sibling, the death of a pet or grandparent. Filtering those emotions through the characters and storyline of a book can help both of you to learn to cope.

When you sit together to read a good picture book that reflects your child's life and emotions, your child begins to deal with his feelings. The big bad wolf can huff and puff, but the baby can tolerate the danger because he is cuddled up with you. Perhaps the big bad wolf symbolizes fear of the scary unknown, from the dark night sky to baby's own poorly understood impulses. By sharing the book, you are educating him about his feelings. As he empathizes with the characters, he is expanding and understanding his emotional repertoire. He learns that small creatures overcome scary situations and triumph. It's right there, in his hands, in his book.

I Love You, I Hate You: Ambivalent Feelings

Ambivalence defines life with a baby and toddler. A parent may never have loved anyone quite so intensely as her new baby, nor felt such impotent, incoherent fury after weeks of sleepless nights or hours of colicky screaming. A baby or a toddler loves nothing more than his parents. He's totally, utterly dependent on them for physical and emotional nurturing. But sometimes they don't do exactly what he wants! Maybe some of those screams come from the shock of being angry at the ones he loves most.

A baby's emotions are just as complicated as yours, and looking for books to help him work through his feelings requires an understanding that those feelings don't come in neat little packages. When he's frightened he may also be excited or sad. Anger begets confusion and sadness, as well as, perhaps, a feeling of power. Sometimes it's easiest to look at emotions in the context of the issues that create them. Books that help describe the most common issues, like separation, may also apply to other feelings and emotions. For a specific concern or interest, like divorce, adoption, or illness, you can consult your local librarian, who can guide you through their collections, or the fabulous *A to Zoo* reference book. On the Internet, check out www.teachingbooks.net for helpful links to many book resources.

Separations: Planning Together for Being Apart

We all have definite feelings about separation. From the moment the umbilical cord is cut, separation from mother and from family is inevitable and constant. From naptime to day care, from bedtime to the death of Grandma, from the big kids going to school to the whole family moving houses, separations are going to happen to your child.

Reading Together about Being Apart

- *Owl Babies,* Martin Waddell, Patrick Benson (illus.). Perhaps the ultimate book on separation anxiety, three siblings deal with their mother's surprising absence in the night.

- *Mama Always Comes Home,* Karma Wilson, Brooke Dyer (illus.). Every bird, cat, and mole mommy leaves her baby but comes back. The implication is clear that your baby's will too.

- *The Kissing Hand,* Audrey Penn. Putting a kiss into the palm of your brave young child before he goes to school is a good coping strategy for separations.

- *The Runaway Bunny,* Margaret Wise Brown, Clement Hurd (illus.). This toddler version of a romantic, chivalric poem affirms a mother's love: My love is so deep that if you go away, I'll follow right behind. (Also *El Conejito Andarín.*)

- *Oh My Baby, Little One,* Kathi Appelt, Jane Dyer (illus.). A book almost as much for you as for the baby, about how Mama bird misses Baby when they're apart.

The feelings connected to these separations can trigger a sense of loss, or even of abandonment. These are profound feelings. They may influence the reunions too. The baby may ignore you when you pick him up from the babysitter, or even scream when you return home from work or shopping. Or like the smallest owlet in Owl Babies, he may never let on that he was anxious, and appear as happy during your absence as on your return. Parents have feelings about separation too. How do you manage your own feelings of separations as your kids grow and leave? Newly delivered mothers generally cope with this fundamental loss by intense nurturing of their newborns. The baby understands at some infantile level that he is cared for, that he is loved. He sees and feels as much as he can at this stage and progressively learns more about his own abilities and himself with an adoring parent's attention. It's the start of a lifetime of communicating and relating on very deep levels.

Charlotte's Top Ten

These days when Charlotte (eighteen-months) can't sleep, instead of asking for milk or mama she plaintively cries for "booky," hoping against hope that we'll turn on the light and read. Often we do because it's the only thing that calms her down. Even in less stressful moments, Charlotte loves to read. She sits and looks at books on her own, pointing out things she recognizes and she'll sit and be read to for longer than she'll do just about anything else. Charlotte is pretty fickle about books; she'll love a particular book for a few weeks and then, like that, drop it for something new. Some books she's rejected since the moment I've brought them home. If I pick up a book she doesn't want she says NO adamantly and pushes it away. She asks for books by name, and I better produce it immediately or watch out. These days she seems to prefer bigger books with a simple story rather than board books, but as I said her tastes change pretty radically every few weeks. Here are the current favorites: —Jane

1. Maisy Goes Shopping (and all of the other paperback Maisy books)
2. There's a Wocket in My Pocket
3. I Can Do It Too
4. Please, Baby, Please
5. There's a Monster at the End of This Book
6. Eat Up, Dudley!
7. Five Little Monkeys with Nothing to Do
8. Miss Spider's Tea Party and Miss Spider's New Car
   (though she's always hated Little Miss Spider)
9. Green Eggs and Ham
10. Baby's Bedtime and Baby's Mealtime (Usborne)

Of course a mother wants a child to move on and go to day care, elementary school, and college. But we also want them to stay right here in our arms. Similarly, even the most loving child sometimes wants nothing more than to move away from his parents and have more grown-up experiences and adventures without a mother hovering behind. But the very idea can be terrifying. Books like *Alice in Wonderland*, *Peter Pan*, *Charlotte's Web*, *Stuart Little*, *Babar*, *Bambi*, *The Lion, the Witch, and the Wardrobe*, *The Wizard of Oz*, *The Secret Garden*, and the *Harry Potter* books are safe ways of trying it out.

The good news is that these books exist for younger children as well, with richly imagined characters who have real feelings and grow to know more about their needs and capacities. Seeing a fictional character endure and triumph fortifies a child for separations of his own.

"My two-year-old godson Malcolm was visiting from New Hampshire. His parents left me in charge of him for the evening, one of the first times he had been left with a sitter. Of course I was prepared with books from the library! Malcolm was fussy that night and cried and seemed to miss his parents. I pulled out Go Away, Big Green Monster, *and we read it over and over and over again. He would shout 'G'Way!' at the top of his lungs at the appropriate moments. I think we read it twenty times that night. It was the only thing that distracted him. That book helped him get through his separation anxiety. A couple of months later, I gave him the book for Christmas. After he ripped off the wrapping paper and saw the cover, his face lit up. He ran over to me immediately, and we read it together. We made a strong personal connection through that book." —Rachel*

The Bedtime Parting

For babies, bedtime is another form of separation. Toddlers may understand that morning will come, but even two-year-olds have some trouble with why they have to go to sleep without you! A baby quickly develops myriad techniques for keeping the parent with him, from the marvelous litanies of "good-nights" in the venerable *Goodnight Moon* to the demand "I want to hear one book more" in *How Do Dinosaurs Say Goodnight?* Best to start now with getting bedtime techniques down pat, since you've got plenty of bedtimes to come.

Thirteen Books for Bedtime Troubles

1. ***Good Night,*** Alfie Atkins, Gunilla Bergstrom, Elisabeth Kallick Dyssegaard (translator). After tireless catering to endless requests, Daddy falls asleep exhausted on the living room floor.

2. ***I Don't Want To Go To Bed,*** Tony Ross. This English artist's princess is a kid we're glad isn't ours...today. She's a powerful little person.

3. ***It's Bedtime, Wibbly Pig!,*** Mick Inkpen. But let us count the ways Wibbly Pig delays the inevitable!

4. ***Bear's Bedtime Wish,*** Ellen Weiss, Joe Ewers (illus.). This is additionally entertaining because Bear likes to go to bed, and these pages can glow in the dark.

5. ***Snug in Mama's Arms,*** Angela Shelf Medearis. This mother soothes and settles down her overtired tot.

6. ***It's Too Soon!,*** Nigel McMullen. Gramps and grandbaby Anna fall asleep together after he follows her routines.

7. ***Good Night, Harry,*** Kim Lewis. A stuffed elephant has trouble falling asleep, unlike his two companions.

8. ***Goodnight, Goodnight, Sleepyhead,*** Ruth Krauss, Jane Dyer (illus.). This gentle toddler's goodnights to her stuffed animals and day could help soothe your baby to sleep.

9. ***Llama, Llama, Red Pajama,*** Anna Dewdney. Mama's read a story and turned out the light, and where is she? When he calls and she doesn't immediately return, baby llama begins to wail in this little drama every parent will recognize. The big bold pictures and the way baby llama's stuffed llama echoes his every expression are charming.

10. ***Go-Go Baby!,*** Roxane Orgill, Steven Salerno (illus.). A modern mama and an older daughter race around the world on a shopping trip to keep up with their sleepless baby in his stroller.

11. ***Chicken Bedtime Is Really Early,*** Erica S. Perl, George Bates (illus.). Bright farm backgrounds get dimmer as it gets later, and more and more of the animals are off to bed. Chicken bedtime is early and hamsters' is late, but everyone's up at dawn when the rooster crows.

12. ***Baby BeeBee Bird,*** Diane Redfield Massie, Steven Kellogg (illus.). Silence settles over the noisy zoo, until BEEBEEBOBBIBOBBIBEEBEEBOBBIBOBBI! The animals will have to teach the Baby BeeBee Bird what night is for before anyone will sleep. Especially great for families with a new baby who's not exactly sleeping on schedule.

13. ***Joshua's Night Whispers,*** Angela Johnson, Rhonda Mitchell (illus.). What's a little boy to do when afraid of noises in the night? Dad is reassuringly available. (Also *Joshua by the Sea; Mama Bird, Baby Bird; Rain Feet.*)

Death and Dying, the Ultimate Separation

Death, of course, is the most permanent loss, but it's also part of life. Although you might have an instinct to shield young children from this reality, if your family is dealing with a death—of a pet, a friend, or a relative—it's better to address it than to have him coming up with his own ideas, which are bound to include the idea that this is not a safe subject to talk about. Once again, a good book can help to create a framework for talking and for understanding.

Five Books to Help Discuss Death

1. ***Nana Upstairs & Nana Downstairs,*** Tomie dePaola. This is a gentle but clear story about losing a grandmother.

2. ***The Old Dog,*** Charlotte Zolotow, James Ransome (illus.). The inevitable tears and sadness at the death of a pet are treated as appropriate and expected. A very honest, sympathetic, artfully painted picture book.

3. ***Frog and the Birdsong,*** Max Velthuijs. Out-of-print but worth searching out, this is a very simple and accepting description of death, prompted by the discovery of a dead bird. From an award-winning Dutch artist.

4. ***When a Pet Dies,*** Fred Rogers, Jim Judkis (illus.). Mr. Rogers offers a comforting way of talking and thinking about this huge permanent loss in a child's (and parent's) life.

5. ***The Tenth Good Thing About Barney,*** Judith Viorst, Erik Blegvad (illus.) Since the '60s this trusty book has helped families deal with a child's grief over the death of a pet cat.

Growing, Changing Families

For all the angst surrounding separation from family, there is a fair bit of struggle involved in being a part of a family as well. Who are these people? What do they do with the baby? What happens if another baby comes along?

The family is a young child's universe: his academy for learning, his laboratory for experimenting, and the mirror in which he sees himself. Books abound that describe and celebrate baby's growing awareness of himself in relation to his family, helping him learn their names and the names of other things and places in his life.

Baby and Family

- ***A Teeny Tiny Baby,*** Amy Schwartz. A family introduces their newborn to his family and neighborhood.

- ***Bubba and Beau Meet the Relatives,*** Kathi Appelt. This funny book demonstrates that even tiny babies have excellent, if messy, skills for meeting new family members.

- ***I Like Me!,*** Nancy L. Carlson. This is a celebration for a young piglet with a wonderfully positive self-image.

- ***Hooray for Me!,*** Remy Charlip, Lillian Moore, and Vera B. Williams (illus.). Here we have a child understanding his relationship to siblings and cousins. (Ms. Williams, as we have said before, puts babies front and center and gives three of them gorgeous fun with various relatives in *"More More More," Said the Baby.*)

- ***My New Baby,*** Annie Kubler. This wordless board book is full of scenes from the life of this newly expanded family.

Mom! The Center of Baby's Universe

In many books, mothers represent the perfect ideal of a supportive presence, always there, always reassuring, a bulwark of love. But sometimes mothers aren't quite so perfect (gasp!) and babies and toddlers need to see this represented in books, too. In books and in life, mothers (and children) can be frustrated and loving at the same time.

Moms, Perfect and Not-So!

- **My Mom,** Anthony Browne. Here's a big-faced appreciation of one mom.

- **Mama, Do You Love Me?,** Barbara Joosse. The mom's answer for her Inuit daughter is always yes, even though the child is a handful.

- **You Are My Perfect Baby,** Joyce Carol Thomas, Nneka Bennett (illus.). Here's one mommy totally in love with her baby. Everything the baby does (like wiggling her toes) as depicted in lovingly soft illustrations is perfect.

- **Momma's Magical Purse,** Paulette Bogan. A mother cat has everything in her capacious bag, including a sense of humor.

- **Grump,** Janet S. Wong, John Wallace (illus.). This rare book captures a very tired, frumpy, grumpy mommy with a boundlessly energetic baby. The illustrations get it right, reflecting something we have all experienced but rarely seen on paper.

- **Olivia,** Ian Falconer. Olivia's mother heaves what is clearly a sigh at the end of a long day and tells Olivia, "You know, you really wear me out. But I love you anyway." And Olivia gives her a kiss back and says, "I love you anyway, too."

- **And My Mean Old Mother Will Be Sorry, Blackboard Bear,** Martha Alexander. A small boy is so fed up with his yelling mother that he escapes into the woods with his imaginary protector bear. The difficulties he experiences help him choose to return…to his small and actual teddy bear.

Daddy

More Daddy books are appearing every day and few of the dads are just carrying a briefcase. Dads dance and sing, play and cook, and generally have fun with their children.

Daddy: The Modern Version

- **Baby Dance,** Ann Taylor. Daddy and baby dance around while Mama naps. The drawings make it really joyous.

- **Papa's Song,** Kate McMullan, Jim McMullan (illus.). Papa Bear takes his sleep-resistant baby to hear the sounds and feel the gentle rhythms of the river.

- **Daddy Makes the Best Spaghetti,** Anna Grossnickle Hines. This is a very engaged and fun-loving daddy with his preschooler. He not only shops and cooks, he's Bathman.

- **Mama's Coming Home,** Kate Banks, Tomek Bogacki (illus.). Mama's crazy commute is shown on one side of the page, Dad's juggling of dinner prep and the witching hour on the other. Nice for families where this is a regular event.

- **What Dads Can't Do,** Douglas Wood, Doug Cushman (illus.). The things dads can't do somehow correlate to those things dads have to do: dads can't cross the street without holding hands, or sleep late, or hold on to their money. Wry illustrations reveal both sides of the story.

- **Vroomaloom Zoom,** John Coy. In a twist on the usual daddy-putting-baby-to-bed theme, this daddy zooms around adventurously in his yellow car with an I-can't-sleep daughter Carmela. It's noisy and fun, and one suspects that Mommy might do things differently.

- **Daddy's Girl,** Garrison Keillor, Robin Preiss Glasser (illus.). This volume of daddy-daughter antics looks and feels real to us. Includes a CD to enjoy.

Families Come in All Varieties and Languages

Families come in all colors, sizes, and shapes, and no matter who's a part of yours, you'll find a book to mirror it back to your baby. Since many families speak more than one language, local bookstores are beginning to stock some books in languages other than English or Spanish. Your local public library may have an even greater selection available.

Books for Families of All Sizes and Stripes

- **Black Is Brown Is Tan,** Arnold Adoff, Emily Arnold McCully (illus.). This interracial family has all these shades and celebrates them all.

- **Hello, Lulu,** Caroline Uff. Lulu the chubby-cheeked little girl introduces us to everyone and everything she loves. Words recur often, making this just the right text for toddlers. (Watch for more Lulu titles if you and your baby like this one.)

- **I Love Saturdays y Domingos,** Alma Flor Ada, Elivia Savadier (illus.). A bilingual girl has twice the fun visiting her two sets of grandparents. It's a colorful celebration of lives and cultures.

- **A Mother for Choco,** Keiko Kasza. After being seen as too different from a mother giraffe and a mother penguin, this orphaned bird fits right in to Mrs. Bear's inter-species family.

- **Louie's Search,** Ezra Jack Keats. A boy's dream of having a father is wonderfully rewarded. The drawings are Keats's usual collage style that amounts to more than the pieces.

- **Joy!,** Joyce Carol Thomas, Pamela Johnson (illus.). This joyous board book features the love a mom has for her child.

- ***The Hello, Goodbye Window,*** Norton Juster, Chris Raschka (illus.). The ins and outs of grandparents enjoying play with their granddaughter through the kitchen window.
- ***Everywhere Babies,*** Susan Meyers, Marla Frazee. We've mentioned this wonderful book before, but its illustrations, depicting every imaginable kind of family, make it worth including here too.

And Baby Makes…Change, Trouble, Fun?

Anticipation and arrival of a new baby brings major changes to the family as a whole. Before baby's arrival, most younger children are excited about the change. Books can help them to have realistic expectations (many expect a much older, more active baby than the one they actually get). After the baby arrives, the worries start, and there's a whole subset of books illustrating the jealousy, irritation, and fear of being pushed aside that might help.

Try to read some books that give a realistic view of life with a new baby. We all have a tendency to talk about how much fun it will be to have a new sibling, and you may find your child is expecting a much older baby and has big— and unrealistic—plans.

"When I was expecting Lily, I went a little overboard and brought home a stack of 'new baby' books. After a day or two of this, when I sat down with Sam and suggested we read, he took one look at the baby book in my lap and shook his head. 'I want a REAL book,' he said." —KJ

Waiting for Baby

- **Baby, Come Out!,** Fran Manushkin, Ronald Himler (illus.). Tapping toes won't make the baby leave the womb. Impatience is handled cleverly and lovingly.

- **Little Brown Bear and the Bundle of Joy,** Jane Dyer. What will it be, this bundle of joy? Luckily, the big brother learns that he's the BIG bundle of joy as he changes into a sibling.

- **It's Quacking Time,** Martin Waddell, Jill Barton (illus.). It's mostly a quiet book about waiting for THAT big blue egg in Mama's nest to crack. It's ducks and eggs, yes, and it's wonderful.

- **I'm a Big Brother,** Joanna Cole, Maxie Chambliss (illus.). What can the big brother or big sister do with the new baby? Lots of wonderful family activities. (Also *I'm a Big Sister*.)

- **Waiting for Baby,** Annie Kubler. Wordlessly we watch a small child begin to understand his mother's pregnancy.

- **What's Inside?** Jeanne Ashbe. Flaps hide the insides of things we can open, things we shouldn't, and things we can't—mama's belly, full of baby, shown getting bigger and bigger. Nice in it's not-wholly-new-baby focus for kids who may have heard enough about the coming events.

But I Thought I'd Like the Baby!

- **Julius, the Baby of the World,** Kevin Henkes. Big sister Lilly's disgust ends only when a visitor criticizes her baby. Then Lilly takes possession of the Baby of the World, befitting her own royal status.

- **On Mother's Lap,** Ann Herbert Scott, Glo Coalson (illus.). Despite the older child's insistence on bringing everything he values onto mother's lap, there's still room for him and the baby.

- **We Have a Baby,** Cathryn Falwell. These parents offer wonderful role modeling for helping a toddler-aged sibling feel loved in the presence of a new baby.

- **Za-Za's Baby Brother,** Lucy Cousins. A big sib zebra deals with feeling neglected because of a new baby's arrival.

- **I Was Born to Be a Sister,** Akaela S. Michels-Gualtieri, Marcy Dunn Ramsy (illus.). A genuine sixth-grade girl writes about having a baby brother, the fun of being with him, and the relief of going off to school.

- **Peter's Chair,** Ezra Jack Keats. Peter has to give up his crib for the new baby, and he has clear feelings about, against, and then for it.

- **Oonga Boonga,** Frieda Wishinsky, Carol Thompson (illus.). The older brother Daniel's made up words distract baby Louise. Very clever story and artwork.

- **Now We Have a Baby,** Lois Rock. Learning to cope with the new baby, with patience and interest, some quiet and love.

- ***What Shall We Do with the Boo Hoo Baby?,*** Cressida Cowell, Ingrid Godon (illus.). Every cow, cat, and duck offer suggestions for soothing this wide-mouthed wailer. The ultimate suggestion may come from pure exhaustion all around.

- ***What Baby Wants,*** Phyllis Root, Jill Barton (illus.). This crying baby is surrounded by well-intentioned family members who want to help look after the baby while Mama takes a nap. However, the baby yowls until the understanding little brother cuddles, kisses, and sings the baby back to peace.

- ***Ella and the Naughty Lion,*** Anne Cottringer, Russell Ayto (illus.). With the new baby's arrival comes a terrible lion, pushing the baby out of his crib and tearing up his toys while big sister protests. The text and the illustrations never concede that the lion is big sister Ella, leaving children to enjoy the idea of conquering jealousy as an outside foe.

- ***Hello Benny: What It's Like to Be a Baby,*** Robie H. Harris, Michael Emberley (illus.). A helpful, lighthearted insight into baby life includes different levels of text to be read as appropriate to a new big brother or sister. There are helpful insights for the parents as well.

- ***Go! Go! Maria! What It's Like to be 1,*** Robie H. Harris, Michael Emberley (illus.). Like *Hello Benny* above, *Go! Go! Maria!* offers a terrific insight into the activities of a one-year-old giddy with her abilities to move about. It's likely to be read to the older child who may not be quite so pleased with the newly mobile, destructive force around the house.

Brothers & Sisters: Can't Live With or Without Them

Siblings constitute another enormous category. Being a sister or brother brings with it rich rewards and many battles. There's getting a brother or a sister, and then there's actually being one, which is a whole different ball game. Books generally handle the crisis in a benign way; the frustrations give way to some good fun and playtime.

Books for Brothers and Sisters

- *Big Brother, Little Brother,* Penny Dale. How do two brothers manage their jealousy and anger when fighting over a toy truck?

- *Do Like Kyla,* Angela Johnson. A big sister deals with her little sister's copycat ways.

- *Do You Know What I'll Do?,* Charlotte Zolotow, Javaka Steptoe (illus.). A sister's affection for her baby brother emerges charmingly as she dreams about doing things for his pleasure.

- *Squashed in the Middle,* Elizabeth Winthrop, Pat Cummings (illus.). Daisy's courage surprises her family into finally understanding how she feels as a middle child longing to be heard.

- *Baby Bear's Chairs,* Jane Yolen, Melissa Sweet (illus.). Being the youngest has some clear advantages, like Dad's lap and parental attention after the others get put to bed. Nice reworking of the three bears and chairs trope.

- *Annie Rose Is My Little Sister,* Shirley Hughes. One of many books starring little Alfie, this Shirley Hughes story depicts siblings interacting realistically. As ever, her artwork is warmly authentic.

> *"With three older siblings, one eight-year-old and two five-year-olds, my nine-month-old baby has quickly adapted to the whole family piling on the bed at night and reading books together. We still read classic board books like* Goodnight Moon *and* Is Your Momma a Llama?, *but we also read lots of nonfiction books about animals and American history. The baby loves it. He focuses for brief moments, looks at the pictures, crawls around between us, and, quite often, grabs a book page and gobbles it up. He's so hungry for words."* —Bruce

Frustration, Anger, and Tantrums

Frustrations are a big part of life for a baby and toddler. Obstacles abound as they try to achieve the simplest of goals: asking for a bottle, pouring milk on cereal, and grabbing that tempting coffee cup off the dinner table. Their lack of language and skill thwarts them; you thwart them. The question becomes what to do with that frustrated, thwarted feeling. The answer isn't always pretty, and tantrums are a part of life with a small child.

Teaching appropriate ways to experience and express anger is one of many tasks of being a parent. Talking to your infant, guessing at what might be bothering him, can help. Telling yourself to count to ten, and teaching your child to do so as well, may be one of the most healthy and helpful things you can do, but meanwhile, a tantrum has to be dealt with.

Six Screaming, Tantrummy, Let-It-All-Out Books

1. **Where the Wild Things Are,** Maurice Sendak. Max goes wild at dinnertime. Banished to his room, he takes an imaginative journey to the island of wild things, where he realizes he'd rather be home and loved and fed than be wild. This offers the clearest representation of a temper tantrum we know.

2. **When Sophie Gets Angry—Really Really Angry...,** Molly Bang. When Sophie gets angry her rage is gloriously, colorfully, and even violently illustrated, and the art calms down with her mood after she gets herself away from the sister who's made her so crazy.

3. **Mean Soup,** Betsy Everitt. Horace is having a very bad day, so his mother cooks up a soup to soothe his frustrations. Once again the artwork helps describe the emotional stew.

4. **Too Loud Lily,** Sofie Laguna, Kerry Argent (illus.). There's a way to channel all that noise! Let's put Little Lily Hippo on the stage.

5. **Angry Dragon,** Thierry Robberecht, Phillipe Goossens (illus.). When Mom says NO, this little guy does become a dragon. When the full-blown episode passes, his parents still love him.

6. **If I Were a Lion,** Sarah Weeks, Heather M. Solomon (illus.). Here's the inner life of the angry kid in the time-out chair. We always wondered what she was thinking.

Tantrums can be as scary and upsetting for a child as they are for the adult. Regardless of the reason for the tantrum, you will have to handle it. Ensuring your child's physical safety is paramount. How you cope will depend on the child and the circumstances. Sticking with him through this terrible moment in his life communicates your support and sends a message about coping. You're still there. That says he can be angry and still be loved. You're trying to help. That says problems are things that can be solved. You're trying to soothe. That says that problems are better solved when the huge surge of anger has passed. Whatever you say, and however you cope with the tantrum at the time, eventually it will pass. He'll collapse, exhausted and spent, into your arms, and you'll move on.

Get out a tantrum book after a tantrum, and use it to talk about how reasonable it is to be angry, and to suggest different ways of dealing with it that wouldn't have been so hurtful or destructive. It may not seem like your words mean much to so young a child, but you may achieve more than you know.

Friends: Real, Imaginary, Stuffed, and All

Babies branch out from their families and start making friends in many ways. Some start with the so-called "transitional object": the binky, the blankie, the filthy remnants of a stuffed dog. Those are treasured possessions, and (with the exception of the binky) usually stick around when real friends start to appear.

Binkys, Blankies, and Stuffies: Books about First Friends

- **Knuffle Bunny: A Cautionary Tale,** Mo Willems. This is an excellent (and funny) depiction of the gulf in understanding between the baby and her daddy about the importance of a stuffed animal that's disappeared. This baby means business!

- **I Lost My Bear,** Jules Feiffer. There is no better illustration of a perfect SCREAM than Feiffer's drawing of the girl when she realizes her bear is missing!

- **Owen,** Kevin Henkes. Owen's clever mother invents a way to preserve her young mouse's personal need for his oversized blanket when he goes to school by creating small pocket-sized ones to carry discretely.

- **Binky and Blankie,** Leslie Patricelli. These two separate board books feature a diapered toddler's life with his beloved transitional objects.

- **Pippo Gets Lost,** Helen Oxenbury. Part of Oxenbury's Tom and Pippo series, this story dramatizes how much losing a sacred object means and reveals about a child's inner emotional capacity to love and cope.

As your baby grows into a toddler and preschooler, his neighbors or companions from music class, day care, or the mommy-baby group will become playmates. They may start by staring at each other. Soon they'll be grabbing for each other's noses, hands, feet, and toys. Toddlers begin by playing next to each other (called parallel play) and progress from there. Those first actual conversations between the new friends are an odd experience—your little baby, talking and relating in a way that doesn't involve you.

These new relationships offer opportunities to learn about relating to another person outside of the immediate family, and it's not always clear sailing. Sharing and being together is tough. There may be bites, sulks, screams, and squabbles over nothing, but it could still be the beginning of a genuine long-term friendship.

Some Favorites about Friends!

- **Best Friends for Frances,** Russell Hoban. This beloved badger Frances offers clever maneuverings when dealing with friends.

- **Two Girls Can,** Keiko Narahashi. These little girl pals show a genuine range of feelings and activities.

- **Will I Have a Friend?,** Miriam Cohen, Lillian Hoban (illus.). Little Jim innocently asks his dad this question on their way to his first day of school. Little ones who worry about having friends will find solace in this gentle reassuring book that's been around for years.

- **My Friend Rabbit,** Eric Rohmann. There's gentle trouble when friends mouse and rabbit play with a favorite airplane toy.

- **Frog and Toad Are Friends,** Arnold Lobel. This is one of several volumes of rich stories about two good friends. A classic.

- **Buster,** Denise Fleming. Can a dog have a cat friend? Of course the answer is yes, although this pointy-nosed scaredy dog has to overcome his original fears of this fluffy white kitten who purrs at him.

- **Mine's the Best,** Crosby Bonsall. Two boys meet carrying identical balloons...and argue over whose is better.

- **Let's Be Enemies,** Janice May Udry, Maurice Sendak (illus.). Not surprisingly, being friends is better—but the journey there is cute and classic.

Hey! You Sat on Pete!
(Very Real Books about Imaginary Friends)

- **When the Sun Rose,** Barbara Berger. A beautiful friendship between a little girl in her playhouse and a friendly lion playmate from her imagination. Beautiful artwork and story.

- **I Have a Friend,** Keiko Narahashi. A boy inventively plays with his shadow's many guises.

- **Jimmy Lee Did It,** Pat Cummings. We all wish we had our own Jimmy Lee when the milk spills, the vase breaks, or things go wrong.

- **Blackboard Bear,** Martha Alexander. A chalk drawing of a bear climbs down and accompanies a small boy, helping him feel more powerful.

- **Leaf Man,** Lois Ehlert. Once read, we can all create "friends" who live in nature, take imaginary journeys, and come home with us.

"My daughter Alice, three, has an older friend Anya, five, and Alice ADORES Anya. Sometimes Anya can get bossy or mean and makes Alice feel bad that she is smaller and can't write her name, or hang upside-down on the monkey bars. It makes Alice feel sad and she gets angry and will act out against Anya. The Dream, a story in Arnold Lobel's Frog and Toad Together, really helped Alice understand her own feelings toward Anya and it built a vocabulary for us to use as a family to discuss these kinds of situations. (Toad dreams that he is the greatest and most exceptional person, pianist, and aerialist. But as he becomes greater, his friend Frog shrinks into insignificance. As the crushed Frog starts to leave, Toad realizes how much he needs his friend Frog, and is relieved to wake up.) Now if someone is really overwhelming Alice, I whisper in her ear, 'Do you feel like you're shrinking?' She'll say yes, then I'll smile and tell her, 'Remember, it's only a dream.' This reminds her of the story and she is able to have a moment of perspective about her situation." —Jane

That's Funny!

Babies and parents all need a good giggle. Life is full of funny things and laughter helps all of us to relax and even to enjoy some of the more boring or difficult parts of caring for (or being) small children. Sharing a laugh is a welcome and gorgeous feeling. Babies actually laugh as early as two or three months. But what makes them laugh? What is funny to a baby and toddler?

IRRESISTIBLE AUTHORS   SANDRA BOYNTON

Almost every mom we talked to listed one of Boynton's colorful, hippo-filled books as a funny favorite. Push the greeting cards right out of your head; everybody has to start somewhere. *Red Hat, Green Hat* is wonderful for all the getting-dressed jokes it creates (the squirmy toddler who won't let you put a shirt over his head will dissolve in giggles if you try to put the shirt on his feet instead), *Barnyard Dance* has wonderful dancing farm animals, and *Hippos Go Berserk* features clever counting and a riotous party.

Very little babies laugh at stimulating motion, tickling, or bouncing on the knee. As they get bigger, both babies and toddlers tend to like silly sounds, goofy faces, and slapstick. A raspberry on the tummy, a big donkey "hee-haw," crossing your eyes, or balancing a slice of bread on your nose might all bring on the giggles. Babies make jokes, too. At nine months, Lily puts her toys into KJ's mouth, and then laughs and laughs, every time. Once the baby laughs, you will find yourself laughing too. Then, because you are laughing, your baby will laugh some more. Laughter is infectious.

{ *"Every morning in my two-year-old classroom we put up a felt board with a schoolhouse on it, and each child gets a felt person to put on the board. When we start to learn some directional terms, I turn the house the wrong way: put it upside down, or on its side, and they laugh and laugh. They know how the house should be, and they know I know, so anything else just tickles them."* —Karen }

A cat that barks is very funny, if you know that a cat really says meow. Toddlers who are just learning who says what will be delighted when the world of "Old MacDonald" is turned upside down. Kids learn fast and may actually crack themselves up with language jokes, some of which are on the order of the cat saying bowwow, or the cow saying oink, or endlessly repeating a word, product, or place.

Building an expectation that then gets upended is funny. Culmination stories or pile-ups offer a crescendo of tension and a welcome relief. Every page has basically the same information, but by the end something's gotta give.

Being contrary is really funny too, starting with babies as young as nine months. In real life it might express a certain inclination towards mischievousness, independence, or even defiance. But stubborn refusal in a picture book is just plain funny. Furthermore it's very funny to hear the adult reader acting out such a traditionally kid role.

{ *Laura's son Joey, at two, developed an unaccountable affection for the words "Taco Bell." He'd never been to a Taco Bell, never even eaten a taco, but something about the phrase charmed him. Soon his mirth infected all of his friends, until there was a whole pack of two-year-olds running in circles, all shrieking "Taco Bell! Taco Bell!" To this day, nearly two years later, any of them will dissolve in giggles if you say those two words.* }

The works of Nancy Shaw and Rosemary Wells offer good visual and verbal silliness for most families. These gifted children's book author-illustrators don't seem to write or talk down to any of us, but rather describe immediately identifiable human quirks and experiences that provide us with the gentle humor of recognition.

Given that humor is often personal and unpredictable, it is a difficult task to find books to recommend for everyone. But really humorous books are often funny for young and old. Since young children tend to laugh if an adult is laughing first, and vice versa, we don't need to analyze too closely. Just find a book that tickles your fancy.

Well, WE Think These Are Funny

- *The Cow That Went OINK,* Bernard Most. This funny book is all about what happens when a cow oinks.

- *To Market, To Market,* Anne Miranda, Janet Stevens (illus.). Based on a traditional nursery rhyme, a lady does the shopping for ever larger animals at the supermarket. Everything is oversized, including the humor.

- *Moo, Baa, La La La!,* Sandra Boynton. Barnyard animals sing their songs in a silly, jaunty manner.

- *I Will Not Go To Market Today,* James Marshall. A big chicken, Fennimore B. Buttercrunch, endures endless catastrophes simply trying to obtain more jam for his morning toast and tea.

- *Baby Danced the Polka,* Karen Beaumont, Jennifer Plecas (illus.). It's nap time on the farm, but one un-sleepy baby has a different plan.

- ***My Little Sister Ate One Hare,*** Bill Grossman. Everything the sister eats is gross, except healthy peas that become very funny.

- ***Goodnight Lulu,*** Paulette Bogan. Mama chicken reassures Lulu at bedtime that all sorts of things WON'T happen or that Mama will deal with it.

- ***Thirsty Baby,*** Catherine Ann Cullen, David McPhail (illus.). The exaggeration of a baby who eventually drinks up all the ocean will make most toddlers giggle. McPhail's illustrations are wonderful.

- ***Good Dog, Carl,*** Alexandra Day. Rottweiler Carl's method of taking care of baby is very, very funny.

- ***Don't Let the Pigeon Drive the Bus!,*** Mo Willems. An unreasonable, wheedling pigeon (who just might remind you of a certain child you know, and looks like that child might have drawn him) is determined to drive that bus. Young children will laugh at the absurdity, older ones at the pigeon's begging techniques.

- ***Leonardo, the Terrible Monster,*** Mo Willems. Leonardo is hilariously terrible at being a monster but pretty good at being a friend, and funny to look at on top of it all.

- ***The Monster at the End of This Book,*** Jon Stone, Michael Smollin (illus.). Grover's heard there's a monster at the end of this book, and he's determined to keep the reader from turning the pages. Lovely suspense, as both Grover and the first-time reader forget that Grover is a monster himself. Classic Muppet illustrations.

- ***Bedtime!,*** Christine Anderson, Steven Salerno. If Melanie's too busy to play in the tub, put on her princess pajamas, and hear a bedtime story, her dog is more than ready to stand in. Funny, almost Seussian illustrations.

- ***Tanka Tanka Skunk!,*** Steve Webb. Funny illustrations of an animal band and a deeply silly chant create the toddler humor here.

- ***Froggy Gets Dressed,*** Jonathan London, Frank Remkiewicz (illus.). Frogs may be supposed to sleep all winter, but when this one sees snow, he wants to play in it—but he keeps forgetting key pieces of clothing and having to go in, undress, and do it all over again. When he finally realizes he's forgotten his underwear, he gives up and goes back to bed.

- ***10 Minutes Till Bedtime,*** Peggy Rathmann. As Dad shouts out the countdown warning, a tourist (!) busload of hamsters arrives to observe this nightly ritual. The pictures of the ensuing chaos are Rathmann at her best, and it's hard to imagine that only the boy knows what's going on as the clock ticks towards bedtime.

Ages and Stages:
Emotional Milestones

This chart is a little bit different from those in other chapters. The information here describes a significant issue for each stage of emotional development and what parents can do to facilitate its successful accomplishment.

Newborn	**Issue:** The newborn's basic issue is trust. **Parent Response:** The more you nurture your infant with love, holding, and caregiving, the more you communicate your reliability and trustworthiness to him. Paying attention with books, looks, and words—it's all good.

Sitting	**Issue:** Sitters begin to engage more with the world around them. This includes socializing, and a developing sense of being a separate person and not totally a part of Mommy and Daddy.
	Parent Response: Using books, mirrors, and conversations, you can tell your child who he is and how much you love him.
	Issue: Stranger anxiety (fear of strangers) begins because the baby knows that you are his mommy, his daddy. That stranger isn't you.
	Parent Response: Once this begins, parents need to spend more time smoothing the transition to the new babysitter or babysitting arrangement. Providing a special transitional object from home helps. And of course playing lots of peekaboo—you will leave AND you will come back.
Crawling/Creeping	**Issue:** Age of Exploration. This age brings with it wonderful discoveries as the physical capacities of babies grow and develop. As they practice going away from you, they also return to the security of "home base." Like real explorers, when they find something they give it a name. Their first words in a baby language might include family members, pets, or favorite objects in their world.
	Parent Response: Trust your baby to explore everything by tasting, feeling, manipulating, and exploring objects. Also trust that although he begins to move away from you, he will come back. You can appreciate what he is learning and talk about it with him.

Cruising/Walking	**Issue:** Advanced Age of Exploration. Babies develop an increasing sense of being like grown-ups along with an interest in people outside the family. **Parent Response:** Create a safe environment for them to explore and practice moving around (make the baby safe from furniture, and vice versa) and seek opportunities to be around others.
Talking (a few words)	**Issue:** Beginning of clear independence, when he does things his own way as opposed to parent's way. NO becomes a significant new word to go with his new status. **Parent Response:** Take a deep breath. Create choices as opposed to confrontations: instead of insisting on your book, offer the baby a choice of two.
Talking More	**Issue:** With the growth of his powers to do and be in control of his own self, his own choices, the baby becomes pleased and proud. He will gain in personal competence in many spheres and express his accompanying feelings of joy. **Parent Response:** Give opportunities to succeed and credit his accomplishments. Share your child's glorious pride. **Issue:** A genuine concern that he has broken or wrecked things that cannot be repaired, which may include your love. **Parent Response:** Help him tape up the torn page in the book, or pick up the mess he's caused due to his immature reflexes, dexterity, or speed.

Running (but not talking much)	**Issue:** The Age of Possessiveness (mine!) leads to inevitable conflicts. Conflicts engender frustrations and angry responses. **Parent Response:** Parents can help by talking about frustrations, and praising the good things the baby accomplishes. Putting words onto feelings and difficult situations increases the baby's awareness of how to cope.
Talking ALL THE TIME!	**Issue:** Further developing sense of being separate and competent, and trusting parents' abiding love. They begin to understand that something out of sight is still in the mind. **Parent Response:** To reassure the child of his competence and your presence even though separated, try these ideas: 1) A penny in the pocket like Dumbo's feather as a reminder that He Can Do It AND that you are with him; 2) For extended separations provide a little a calendar on which to check off the days and offer a token gift for each day. **Issue:** Creative and imaginative play grows exponentially as he learns to express himself through the manipulation of toys, and giving his dolls and cars things to say. Through various dress-up games he can pretend to be other people. **Parent Response:** Provide materials for him to use in play (empty cardboard boxes, paper and crayons, glue, and old clothes or costumes).

Chapter Ten:
Books to the Rescue: Potty Training, Food, Big Kid Beds, and More

E ven as she's learning to handle her emotions, a baby or toddler is busily trying to master the rest of our complex world. She's without any cultural context for events ranging from "birthday party" to "doctor's appointment," and she's constantly learning our expectations. Why eat with a spoon? Why NOT drop the food on the floor? And, oh, boy, why do I have to poop in THERE?

Once again, books can help. A few dozen readings about Little Critter's dentist visit or Caillou's first plane ride can help a baby or toddler prepare for the unknown. *Everyone Poops* and *My Big Boy Bed* may smooth those transitions, or at least offer a nonconfrontational place to talk about them.

There are books out there for nearly every milestone or challenge you and your baby might face. There are even whole series dedicated to some of the many firsts ahead like *First Experiences from Fred Rogers* (of *Mr. Rogers' Neighborhood*), the stylish *First Experiences* books published by Usborne, and even *What to Expect Kids*, from the people who brought us *What to Expect When You're Expecting*.

What follows are the best books we could find for going beyond the easy chair: books for the kitchen and bathroom, books for being sick and being well, books that travel on planes, trains, and roller coasters. Don't keep your books cooped up on the shelf. Use them to help both of you solve problems at home and maneuver out in the world.

Once Upon a Potty and Other Bathroom Classics

There will be moments ahead when you believe potty training is going to be a lifelong activity. Fortunately, that's probably an exaggeration—it's only going to feel like a lifetime. For some kids, it's easy, for others, it's a struggle, but all seem to be fascinated by the process (and, when they're a little bit older, all the opportunities for humor that go along with it).

It's tough for a toddler or preschooler to sit still on that potty. Put a basket of books (on any subject) where she can reach them while she's waiting for action.

Most kids potty train somewhere between two and four, and even younger kids are usually interested (and may want to try it out). You'll probably start a book or two on the subject before you actually start making the effort. (If you're potty training a boy, you may want to consider whether you'll be having him pee sitting down or standing up, and check the illustrations accordingly.) As with many milestone books, like moving out of a crib or starting school, you can probably find a potty training book starring one of your child's favorite video friends like Elmo or Grover from *Sesame Street*. You might even find a video or DVD. It never hurts to put a familiar face on a new experience, particularly if it turns out to be something of a struggle for your child. We say, if it makes it easier (or faster) it's worth it!

A Little Potty Reading

- **Everyone Poops,** Taro Gomi. A great place to start, since it's more about the poop itself than exactly where you're supposed to put it.

- **Once Upon a Potty,** Alona Frankel. Truly the genre classic and available, like most potty books, for boys and girls—which, much as we may resist the whole pink/blue dichotomy, is important when it comes to illustrations.

- **A Potty for Me!,** Karen Katz. A joyous whole page lift-the-flap instruction manual.

- **Time to Pee,** Mo Willems. Complete with sticker chart, this is stylish and fun.

- **The Princess and the Potty,** Wendy Lewison, Rick Brown (illus.). Expect giggles when a princess refuses to use even the most fabulous potties the kingdom can produce. Kids and parents alike can benefit from the gentle reminder: the princess, like every child, will use the potty when she's ready.

- **I Want My Potty,** Tony Ross. Continues the royalty theme for the truly princess-mad, and shows that even princesses can make mistakes.

- **Uh Oh! Gotta Go!,** Bob McGrath, Shelley Dieterichs (illus.). Twenty toddlers experience the potty in different ways (standing up, flushing).

- **Underwear Do's and Don'ts,** Todd Parr. Just a funny, no potty-training pressure book about, well, underwear (and why you shouldn't let a hippo try it on).

- **Potty Time,** Guido Van Genechten. Puts animals from elephants to dogs each on her own matching potty.

- **Potty!,** Mylo Freeman. Only the best bottom will fit on this potty. Can you guess whose bottom is best: giraffe, snake, leopard, or a small boy?

Rub a Dub Dub, a Book in the Tub

The potty's not the only thing in the bathroom. You might see the bathtub as a place for getting clean, but your child sees it as place for playtime, bubble time, or pirate time. Sometimes there's a conflict there, but it's usually quickly resolved by a fast scrub down and ample opportunity to play.

Books for (and about) Tub Time

- **Tub Toys,** Terry Miller Shannon. A boy puts so many toys in the tub that "there's hardly room for me!"

- **The Tub People,** Pam Conrad, Richard Egielski (illus.). Addresses that childhood fear of going down the drain as the seven members of a wooden tub family go to the rescue when the tub child slips away.

- **Bubble Bath Pirates,** Jarrett J. Krosoczka. A mother playfully gets her two young kids to have great imaginative fun as pirates in the bath.

- **Big Red Tub,** Julia Jarman, Adrian Reynolds (illus). One little girl shares her bath with lots of imagined animals.

- **Way Down Deep in the Deep Blue Sea,** Jan Peck, Valeria Petrone (illus.). Diving for tub toys turns into quite an imaginary adventure in rhythm.

- **Just Me in the Tub,** Mercer Mayer, Gina Mayer. Little Critter shows all of us how to take a bath, some of which involves putting his guests in order.

- **To the Tub,** Peggy Perry Anderson. A father-son bathtime book full of tolerance for the stalling techniques of the little frog child.

- **Waves in the Bathtub,** Eugenie Fernandes. Kady's bath is oceanic!

- **Bathtub Blues,** Kate McMullan, Janie Bynum. A pack of rowdy, big-headed toddlers don't want to take a bath, but when they do, the Bathtub Blues turn out to be big fun. Bright colors, line drawings, and a CD so everyone can sing along (which might be a mixed blessing).

A Kitchen Full of Books

If reading is nourishment for the mind and food for the body, then reading about food must be especially enriching (and reading about food while eating food is almost too much of a good thing). Food is a favorite subject of many a child, and many a children's author. There are books about cooking it, eating it, growing it, and playing with it. All would be perfect for a little light high-chair reading.

Eating, Learning, and Playing in the Warmest Room in the House

- ***What Pete Ate From A–Z (Really!),*** Maira Kalman. Pete, a dog, eats indiscriminately including an accordion, egg beater, and underpants.

- ***Eat Up, Gemma,*** Sarah Hayes, Jan Ormerod (illus.). This baby is deliciously true to form as she plays with her food.

- ***Little Pea,*** Amy Krouse Rosenthal. Little Pea's parents make him count and eat his candy before he's allowed to enjoy his vegetable dessert.

- ***I Will Never Not Ever Eat a Tomato,*** Lauren Child. Big brother Charlie encourages Lola to eat her mashed potato "clouds" and mermaid sticks from the supermarket under the sea.

- ***First Book of Sushi,*** Amy Wilson Sanger. Fun and funky collage illustrations introduce new foods and make egg tamago, tortillas, and guacamole feel as familiar as pancakes and apples in the World Snacks series. (Also *Hola Jalepeno*.)

- ***Eating the Alphabet,*** Lois Ehlert. The fruits and vegetables are appetizingly described in colorful words and pictures. A modern classic.

- **Now I Eat My ABC's,** Pam Abrams, Bruce Wolf (illus.). The alphabet letter is created out of photographed foods to eat and enjoy. Well done.

- **Pots and Pans,** Patricia Hubbell, Diane deGroat (illus.). A rhythmic chant about what happens when baby's in the kitchen with the pots and pans that ends with a very messy kitchen and a very frazzled daddy.

- **The Saucepan Game,** Jan Ormerod. The baby uses her pot for everything imaginable…except, of course, to cook.

- **Two Eggs, Please,** Betsy Lewin. Every animal patron at the diner orders two eggs, but cooked in every possible different way.

- **Bread, Bread, Bread,** Ann Morris, Ken Heyman (illus.). Photographs of various breads from around the world show how differently we are the same.

- **Yuck!** Mick Manning, Brita Granstrom. What birds and other creatures eat isn't for our baby!

- **Cool as a Cucumber** and **Sweet as a Strawberry,** Sally Smallwood. Photographs and kids comparing new foods to more familiar tastes.

Mealtime with a baby is face-to-face time, and a great time for talking. Food is a great teaching tool, both in the pages of a book and on the plate. For baby, naming foods and talking about their color, shape, and texture is fun. Books that show babies eating messily might make him giggle. Older babies and toddlers will enjoy hungry animals, books about kitchen play, and reading books about a variety of foods, from sushi to tortillas to pancakes.

Someone's in the Kitchen with Mommy

There is no more enthusiastic cooking partner than a toddler or preschooler. This can be great when you need someone to shell peas and not so great if you're trying to put dinner together in a crunch (thus the box of toys and books on the floor!).

For those days when you have time, cooking together is a great activity. It's just messy enough to be fun and there's nothing like the pride that comes with making something other people will enjoy eating. Plus, kids are more likely to try something new if they've had a hand in making it, even if it was just to push the buttons on the food processor.

Most recipes can allow for some toddler participation: pouring in the olive oil or scooping the sugar. As your child gets bigger, she'll be able to do more. If you're interested in recipes that are kid-friendly in the kitchen and at the table, these books should help:

- *Pretend Soup and Other Real Recipes: A Cookbook for Preschoolers and Up,* Mollie Katzen, Ann Henderson.
- *Cooking Art: Easy Edible Art for Young Children,* MaryAnn F. Kohl.
- *The Secret Life of Food* and *Hey There, Cupcake!,* Clare Crespo.
- *Fanny at Chez Panisse: A Child's Restaurant Adventures with 46 Recipes,* Alice L. Waters.
- *Blue Moon Soup: A Family Cookbook,* Gary Goss, Jane Dyer (illus.).
- *Tallulah in the Kitchen,* Nancy Wolff. Both a cookbook and a story.

Toddlers and twos also like counting food, and there's no better way to start subtraction than with cookies. There are a bunch of commercialized brand-name counting books out there that feature various snacks. Whether they are a harmless gimmick or an early introduction to the pervasiveness of brand names and marketing depends entirely on your perspective. We think you'll be counting pastas and crackers and other foods with or without these books.

How Does Your Garden Grow?

Toddlers and two-year-olds are fascinated by the growing process. How can a tiny seed become food? If you have any earth at all, or even just a pot, watching that process happen is a thrill for a child. Sugar snap peas, pumpkins, and carrots are easy to grow from seed. Even growing just a few is exciting. Because the whole thing is such a mystery—even after you see it happen, it's still hard to believe—children usually love even the simplest books about young gardens and gardeners.

Great Books for Little Gardeners

- **Planting a Rainbow,** Lois Ehlert. Mom and her child plant a garden of bulbs and seeds which emerge in glorious half pages with all the flowers labeled.

- **The Ugly Vegetables,** Grace Lin. A young girl is disappointed that her mother has decided to grow ugly Chinese vegetables instead of the flowers their neighbors grow. When the ugly vegetables become delicious soup, all the neighbors want to try it and grow their own.

- **The Carrot Seed,** Ruth Krauss, Crockett Johnson (illus.). A very simple story of a boy who believes his seed will grow in the face of much familial doubt—and he's right!

- **Flower Garden,** Eve Bunting. This flower garden comes in a box and comes home by bus—an urban gardener's story.

- **One Bean,** Anne Rockwell, Megan Halsey (illus.). A young narrator describes what happens when you plant one bean.

- **Jack's Garden,** Henry Cole. This is the garden that Jack built, from planting to sprouting to budding to bloom.

- **Two Old Potatoes and Me,** John Coy, Carolyn Fisher (illus.). A dad and his young daughter rescue more than some sprouty bits of old potatoes to keep things growing.

- **Muncha! Muncha! Muncha!,** Candace Fleming, G. Brian Karas (illus.). Can you out-smart three hungry rabbits who think you planted a garden of vegetables just for them?

- **Whose Garden Is It?,** Mary Ann Hoberman. It's perfect, but does it belong to the bees, the worms, the rabbit, the rain? This garden needs them all to grow.

Clothes! No Clothes!

Getting dressed can be a minefield. Babies don't want to lay on that changing table for one more minute, toddlers are more interested in figuring out how to get their clothes off than letting you put them on, and twos, both boys and girls, often suddenly develop startlingly firm opinions about what they want to wear when. You'll have to pick your battles. There may be some wiggle room about the red shirt with the bicycle on it that she's worn for the last three days, but for much of the year there's no question that she's going to have to wear something. Books about clothes are a great source of inside jokes, and a few good jokes can make a tight shirt go over a little head much more easily.

Get Me Dressed!

- *Ella Sarah Gets Dressed,* Margaret Chodos Irvine. A little girl sticks firmly to her own inimitable style.

- *Under My Hood I Have a Hat,* Karla Kuskin, Fumi Kosaka (illus.). Good story about pieces of clothing and the fun of being all dressed up in winter snow. (For older children see *The Philharmonic Gets Dressed*, Karla Kuskin, Marc Simont (illus.) with instrument cases, suspenders and ruffly shirts.)

- *The Jacket I Wear in the Snow,* Shirley Neitzel, Nancy Winslow Parker (illus.). A cumulative dress-up-for-winter-time tale, starting with the jacket.

- *Sweater,* Kit Allen. A sweater to wear in the crisp fall weather for this funny bald narrator's playtime.

- **Daisy Gets Dressed,** Clare Beaton. Wonderful fabric illustrations show Daisy looking for each item of clothing, and give the reader a chance to pick it out from a group of things on the facing page.

- **Bing: Get Dressed,** Ted Dewan. Bing pees in his pants because it's taken such a long time to dress. Now the getting dressed starts all over again.

- **Jesse Bear, What Will You Wear?,** Nancy Carlstrom. A day's wardrobe for the bear, from pants to shirts to a tight chair to PJs.

- **Which Hat Is That? A Flip-the-Flap Book,** Anna Grossnickle Hines, LeUyen Pham (illus.). Full page flaps give the answers for quite a variety of hats.

The Mess in the House

Kids' rooms are their kingdoms, the one place in the house that's uniquely theirs (and even shared rooms are kid territory). It's easier to leave a little mess on the ground in a room you don't have to walk through on the way to the kitchen, but a room that's been the center of a day of playing and reading is eventually going to need to be cleaned. Babies and toddlers often like helping—any activity that involves putting things into a box works for them—but twos may be more resistant. It only takes a few missing toy pieces and stumbles over the mess on the way to the bathroom in the middle of the night for them to begin to understand why this is important, but they still may not like actually doing it. Books, which usually take both the mess and the cleaning to wild extremes, illustrate both the problem and the many ways that cleaning up can be fun.

- **Max Cleans Up,** Rosemary Wells. Big sister Ruby helps Max clean, but Max reminds her of the importance of leaving a place for his treasures, even if they aren't exactly to her taste.

- **Captain Bob Takes Flight,** Roni Schotter, Joe Cepeda (illus.) Captain Bob "clears his runway" and cleaning up becomes just another game.

- **How Do Dinosaurs Clean Their Room?,** Jane Yolen, Mark Teague (illus.). A number of toddler dinosaurs make attempts to put toys and messes away just like human kids. The major differences have to do with size and names, because the exasperated parents look very human indeed. (Also *¿Cómo Ordenan Sus Habitaciones los Dinosaurios?* and more dinosaur titles.)

- **Tidy Titch,** Pat Hutchins. When young Titch's siblings clean out their old toys, he takes their cast-offs, and suddenly his room is the messy one.

- **Pigsty,** Mark Teague. When his mom said this narrator's room is turning into a pigsty, she might have been joking. However, there are genuinely pigs who inhabit his room, and cleaning it up is both frustrating and grounds for a new friendship.

- **Clean Your Room, Harvey Moon!,** Pat Cummings. This very funny rhymed story is a rendering of the wish to push it all under the carpet. The volume of stuff that Harvey has collected is amazing. Why isn't a literal cover up good enough to outsmart Mom?

My Very Own Bed in My Very Own Room

Some kids are thrilled at the idea of moving into a big kid bed. Others are determined to hang onto their crib forever (a problem if there's a new tenant waiting in the wings). And when it comes time to actually sleep in that new place in the dark, even little ones who originally embraced the idea can be nervous. Moving into one's own room is another huge transition. Toddlers who've been sharing a room with Mom and Dad, a baby, or an older sibling and are about to move can be overwhelmed by the idea of a room of their own. Either is a big transition, and it takes time, patience, and a few nights (or weeks) of interrupted sleep before things settle down. Hearing that he's not the only small person who ever felt this way can help.

Books for Bedtime in a New Bed

- **My Sleepy Room,** Jessica Steinbrenner, Elizabeth Wolf (illus.). Bess, a curly-haired little girl with a stuffed panda bear, tells us all the nice things about her new bedroom.

- **Rosa's Room,** Barbara Bottner, Beth Spiegel (illus.). Rosa has moved to a new house, and she's turning an empty space into her own cozy room.

- **My Big Boy Bed,** Eve Bunting, Maggie Smith (illus.). He's got a baby sib in the crib, so he's exploring all the advantages of his new big boy bed. As parents with children who face this change will note quickly, one of the advantages from the boy's point of view is the ease of getting in and out independently.

- **My Own Big Bed,** Anna Grossnickle Hines, Mary Watson (illus.). A preschooler deals handily with some of the fears (like falling out) that come with the move out of the crib.

- **Big Enough for a Bed,** Apple Jordan, John E. Barrett (illus.). A very short, very simple book. *Sesame Street*'s Elmo leaves his crib, chooses new sheets for his new bed, and gathers all the things he needs to snuggle up for the night. Good for making the crib-bed transition with a less verbal child.

Books in Sickness and in Health

It's sometimes hard to tell what constitutes a new adventure for a child and what makes them anxious. A doctor or dentist visit could do both. Your presence is the ultimate reassurance, but a book can help turn the dentist's chair into a more familiar place before you've even left the house.

Buy your child a doctor's kit to go with a doctor's appointment book. A little role-playing makes appointments easier, and you'll be playing the patient and bandaging stuffed animals for years to come.

Doctor and dentist visits will eventually become part of the routine, but a hospital stay, no matter how serious, is hard for a baby or a child at any age—not to mention his parents. It's overly facile to say that books will help if it feels like nothing can, but books can give both of you something else to occupy yourselves. For a toddler or two-year-old, books on topic are good some of the time, and books that take both of you away to a different place may be even better. A baby will be soothed just by the sound of your voice.

Bumps and Boo-boos, Tummy- and Toothaches (and the People That Make Them All Better)

- **Doctor Maisy,** Lucy Cousins. Maisy wears a white coat to help her ailing friend Panda.

- **Corduroy Goes to the Doctor,** Don Freeman, Lisa McCue (illus.). Corduroy's check-up might reassure and prepare your own little one.

- **Just Going to the Dentist,** Mercer Meyer. Little Critter is brave, and even has a filling.

- **Jonathan Goes to the Doctor,** Susan K. Baggette, William J. Moriarty, (illus.). The illustrations, photos of an actual child at his doctor's office, might go a long way to reduce fear of those unfamiliar instruments, especially for younger babies.

- **Harry and the Dinosaurs Say "Raahh!,"** Ian Whybrow, Adrian Reynolds (illus.). Harry and his bucketful of dinosaurs are a bit nervous about the dentist, but not nearly as nervous as the dentist is about them.

- **Froggy Goes to the Doctor,** Jonathan London, Frank Remkiewicz (illus.). Regular check-ups involve waiting, worries, and some funny exams.

- **Benny,** Sieb Posthuma. A young dog, tiny in the middle of the vast page, loses his sense of smell. How can he do his doggy thing? Fortunately, it's just a cold, and a little doggie TLC soon has him sniffing again.

Books about illness might be scary for young children, even if they have a happy ending. It's okay—in fact, it's good—to have a book that introduces some new ideas. And you're right there with her to talk about it. The combination of you and the book offer a reminder that she can manage or find ways to work around something she finds scary. She can manage being sick and getting better. If your child has a specific medical issue, a web search or a talk with your librarian is likely to turn up books that might help her to understand what's happening.

Get Well Soon Books

- **Felix Feels Better,** Rosemary Wells. Wonderful on all levels. Felix's ailments are fixed by a visit to the doctor and mother's TLC.

- **Goldie Locks Has Chicken Pox ,** Erin Dealey, Hanako Wakiyama (illus.). A funny and completely nonthreatening approach to the itchy spots, as every fairy tale friend sends a characteristic get-well note.

- **Don't You Feel Well, Sam?,** Amy Hest, Anita Jeram (illus.). Cough medicine for this coughing bear, along with extra closeness from his mommy, see him back to health.

- **Guess Who, Baby Duck!** Amy Hest. To help Baby Duck recover his usual healthy spunk, Grandpa and Baby Duck review happier times as they look at a family photo album.

- **Mommies Don't Get Sick!,** Marylin Hafner. Little Abby tries to help her ailing mom and toddler sib by doing household chores. With Dad's help, she does. Both Abby and Dad get high marks. The declarative title might suggest the truth in most households: it's not allowed.

- **The Sick Day,** Patricia Maclachlan, Jane Dyer (illus.). This dad lets his daughter have a day off to get better. Unusual for its comforting simplicity, it's also rare to find a book focused on a single dad and his daughter.

- **Loud Lips Lucy,** Tolya L. Thompson, Juan R. Perez (illus.). Lucy's loud and screamy and now has laryngitis. Colorful and explanatory.

- *Miffy in the Hospital,* Dick Bruna. Starting with a sore throat and not feeling very strong, Miffy goes to the hospital. As usual Dick Bruna's gentle, calm approach and simple artwork comforts all of us.
- *Curious George Goes to the Hospital,* H. A. Rey, Margaret Rey. George the monkey, who swallows a piece of a puzzle, never loses his curiosity amidst all the hospital equipment and staff.

And I Will Read It on a Train and I Will Read It on a Plane

Libraries and bookstores are full of books about planes, trains, and automobiles. In fact, many authors, like Byron Barton (*Planes, Trains, My Car*) and Lois Lenski (*The Little Airplane, The Little Train, The Little Auto*), have written all three. For many kids, it would be tough to find a bad book on any kind of moving machine whether it's planes, trucks, spaceships, or bulldozers. Both boys and girls are fascinated. There must be dozens of books on each of these in every library, and you can always thrill a plane lover, or a train lover, by consulting with the librarian and coming home with a stack of fun books.

Big and little kids traveling together can share the *I Spy* board books. Both can look for the missing objects, and beginning readers may be able to manage the rhymes.

- **Airport,** Byron Barton. A simple walk-through of a trip to the airport and onto a plane, done with typical Barton simple directness.

- **We're Going on an Airplane,** Steve Augarde. Great knobs, snacks, and even the pilot's wheel to play with. (His *Garage* is also good.)

- **Little Red Plane,** Ken Wilson-Max. An interactive book that follows a brief story about the adventurous little red plane.

- **Amazing Airplanes,** Tony Mitton, Ant Parker. A whole airplane voyage for animals, and lots of information for readers about pilots, intercom, snacks, seatbelts, and the bump of the wheels on landing. (The authors' *Cool Cars* and *Amazing Machines* are also very satisfying.)

- **Down in the Subway,** Miriam Cohen, Melanie Hope Greenberg (illus.). Oh how we'd like to be on THIS car, where a magical Jamaican lady transforms a simple ride into an island fiesta. Caribbean rhythms and pictures to match.

- **Trains,** Byron Barton. Wonderfully simplified with journeys and riders and routes.

- **Things That Go,** Anne F. Rockwell. This well-known book is almost a dictionary as it lists and illustrates many obvious wheeled things plus surfboards, space shuttles, and strollers.

- **Miss Mouse Takes Off,** Jan Ormerod. Miss Mouse, a gangly stuffed friend, narrates as she and her little girl take an adventure-filled first plane ride.

- **The Wheels on the Race Car,** Alex Zane, James Warhola (illus.). Truly the book for any kids who've seen NASCAR races zoom by on the little screen and a clever take on "The Wheels on the Bus."

- **I Like Cars,** Richard Morgan, Terry Burton (illus.). A small format toddler-talk-about book is just right for learning and talking all about cars including colors, sizes, and where it goes. (Also *I Like Big Trucks*.)

- **Trucks, Trucks, Trucks,** Peter Sís. Lots of different trucks and the jobs they do, some with fold out pages. Satisfying colors of yellow and white. (Also *Fire Truck*.)

- **My Car,** Byron Barton. Sam has a car. He shows and tells us quite a lot about it.

- **On The Road,** Susan Steggall. Two kids in the backseat of Mama's car really do see a lot as they travel along the city streets into the country roads and to the sea.

Richard Scarry books are perfect for travel, because there's so much going on in each one. Try *Cars and Trucks* and *Things That Go*, or *A Day at the Airport*. There's a story on every page, a continuing story, and recurring characters to search for throughout.

Everyday Outings: To the Grocery Store and Beyond!

Books can take us to exotic places, but sometimes the books that just stick close to home are equally appealing. Books can put a thrill in an everyday outing and remind kids to stay close and keep a good grip on a favorite toy while out in the world.

Little Trips into the Big World

- **Harry and the Bucketful of Dinosaurs,** Ian Whybrow, Adrian Reynolds. Harry loses his friends, but finds that they come when he calls.

- **A Pocket for Corduroy,** Don Freeman. Corduroy gets lost on a trip with Lisa and her mother to the laundromat, all because he has no pocket on his overalls. Lisa is once again a model of compassion.

- **Max's Dragon Shirt,** Rosemary Wells. Max gets lost looking for Ruby in a bunny department store. This book contains some of Ms. Wells's funniest illustrations.

- **The Shopping Basket,** John Burningham. An ordinary trip to the shop becomes an extraordinary adventure for Steven as he encounters all sorts of hazards on his way home and has to use his wits to overcome them.

- **Shoes,** Elizabeth Winthrop, William Joyce (illus.). When babies get shoes, they are prepared for the outdoors in all weathers. Just see where these shoes take them.

- **Baby in a Car,** Monica Wellington. Simple drawings of one out-the-window sight per page take the reader along for the ride.

Get Outside

Books help you to experience winter when the sun is shining or take a trip to the beach while a cold rain falls. Lots of outside activities can be a little intimidating for toddlers. The big kids jump into that water enthusiastically, but lots of little ones are more hesitant. Reading a book about characters learning to ice skate, swim in the ocean, and even going barefoot in the sand can make babies feel braver. Books about hikes, picnics, and parks create a point of reference and make a child's own outside fun even more enjoyable.

Books for the Great Outdoors

- **The Snowy Day,** Jack Ezra Keats. Said to be the first picture book with an African America child protagonist when first published in the 1960s, *The Snowy Day* has achieved its classic, irreplaceable status for all young families because of its simplicity, elegance, and shared delight in watching a small boy explore a snowy day.

- **First Snow,** Bernette G. Ford, Sebastien Braun (illus.). We see a new season through the eyes of a bunny and his siblings.

- **Tom and Pippo at the Beach,** Helen Oxenbury. Tom takes his beloved stuffed Pippo everywhere with him.

- **Spot Goes to the Beach,** Eric Hill. Seeing Spot surrounded by his spotty duck inner tube, carrying his sand pail, and wearing his jaunty hat is a suitable start for another adorable, fun, lift-the-flap toddler treat.

- **Sally Goes to the Mountains,** Stephen Huneck. Sally is a black Lab dog who eagerly explores the sights, smells, and animals on an outing to the mountains with her human. Huneck has also let Sally investigate and enjoy the beach and the farm in other picture books.

- **Blueberries for Sal,** Robert McCloskey. Sal is a little girl who gets lost alongside a baby bear who gets found on an old-fashioned blueberrying expedition. This delightful book captures the sights and sounds of picking blueberries perfectly.

- **Snow Day,** Lynn Plourde, Hideko Takahashi (illus.). Babies don't yet know the absolute delight brought about by the words "snow day," but this book will put them straight immediately. With bright, graphic pictures, we follow a family through a day of snowy activities inside and out.

- **A Lovely Day for Amelia Goose,** Yu Rong. Up in the morning and out to play in the pond with her friend Frog, Amelia has a wonderful day.

As you read even the most ordinary-seeming book to your baby, try to think about how it relates to her day and her world. If she grows used to seeing herself, and her life, reflected and expanded on in books, she'll seek out that experience again and again as she grows up. Books take us out into the world, and they bring the world in to us.

Chapter Eleven:
Reading Happily Ever After

You know reading to your child, as a baby, a toddler, or a two-year-old, can enhance your relationship. If you've been reading together, you've seen how valuable books are: how they calm both of you in times of fatigue and stress, how they add entertainment and conversation to your life together. As you continue to grow and read together, remember to leave special baby favorites on the bookshelf. It's surprising how long they continue to have an important place in your child's life.

As your baby becomes a preschooler, reading only gets better. New picture books will get longer, more elaborate, and extend the range of your children's knowledge into science and nature, fables and fairy tales, humor and jokes. You'll probably want to make even more use of the library, since the phrase "Again! Again!" becomes less frequent and finding new favorites becomes more fun.

Depending on your child, sometime during the third or fourth year you may be able to introduce short chapter books. The earliest ones maintain plenty of artwork, but with expanded text comes a drop in illustrations. Your child's imagination will create its own. New and difficult concepts are absorbed as your child learns to follow the important parts of the story.

As she gets even older, you will find beloved authors and illustrators and watch for their new books to be published together.

> *"This morning I heard the now four-year-old Sam playing on the floor of the kitchen, fully engaged in some sort of flying toy. When I tuned in, I heard him declare, 'My elevator is the fastest ever! We'll go all the way to the Space Hotel!' Evidently* Charlie and the Great Glass Elevator, *even with sparse illustrations, confusing scenes with the president, and scary man-eating Knids, is making inroads on his imagination."* —KJ

Parents of preschoolers worry unnecessarily about when their child will begin to read on her own. Some pointing and sounding out words in books is fine. Soon enough she'll be asking you for that kind of help. But our advice is to keep reading. Too much instruction, too much pressure (and your child will notice what you're doing, guaranteed), and reading isn't fun anymore.

- ***Cloudy with a Chance of Meatballs,*** Judi Barrett, Ron Barrett (illus.). Food falls from the sky in the land of Chewandswallow until the weather takes a turn for the worse in this silly tall tale with plenty of detailed illustrations for poring over.

- ***The Giant Jam Sandwich,*** John Vernon Lord, Janet Burroway (illus.). How to catch a thousand wasps? Capture them in the world's biggest jam sandwich, of course. But it will take helicopters and giant machinery and a really big loaf of bread…all right there on the page to enjoy.

- ***Alice the Fairy,*** David Shannon. Alice is a pretend fairy, not a real fairy, because it's hard to be a real fairy. Rough-and-tumble gap-toothed Alice figures she'll probably be a temporary fairy forever, because although she can turn her dad into a "horse" (for a horsey ride) and a plate of cookies into "mine," she's not ready for all the tests that come with advanced fairy school, and she's happy the way she is.

- ***Zen Shorts,*** Jon Muth. The serene watercolor illustrations come in two styles, Western for the children interacting with their new panda neighbor and more Japanese for the stories he tells—stories that link to the children's everyday problems and provide both a new way of looking at things and, for those who are interested, a brief introduction to Zen philosophy. Whether it's a jumping point for discussion or just a picture book, *Zen Shorts* is both engrossing and visually stunning.

- ***Raising Dragons,*** Jerdine Nolen, Elise Primavera (illus.). The narrator was, she says, born to raise dragons, and when she finds an egg, she does, against a darkly colorful painted backdrop of Pa farming and Ma keeping up the farmhouse. Her dragon proves very useful, and even though he outgrows the farm, he sees to it that she has more dragons to raise before he goes. (Also *The Balloon Farm.*)

- **The Best Pet of All,** David LaRochelle, Hanako Wakiyama (illus.). "No dog," says Mom, but she agrees to a pet dragon, little dreaming that the boy would manage to find one and bring him home. It turns out that dragons, even in a neat, graphic, and colorful world that evokes a nostalgic vision of the fifties, aren't very good pets. How to get rid of this one? Well, it turns out they don't like dogs.

- **The Relatives Came,** Cynthia Rylant, Stephen Gammell (illus.). They came, and they stayed all summer, or so it seemed. All the inconveniences are forgotten in the fun of being a big family squashed together, perfectly captured by hazy, glowing pastel illustrations.

- **How I Became a Pirate,** Melinda Long, David Shannon (illus.). Pirates recruit a young sand-castle builder to join them and dig a hole for their buried treasure, promising to get him back for soccer practice. No vegetables and no manners are great, but this young pirate misses having someone to tuck him in at night. Shannon's characteristically rugged illustrations capture the boy and the pirate band.

- **Alphabet Adventure,** Audrey Wood, Bruce Wood (illus.). This alphabet's been in training, and they're all ready for school—but little i's dot is missing, and everyone joins in the search. Readers can spot the hiding dot in the glossy illustrations and help straighten out the letters as they line up for school once the dot is found.

- **Diary of a Worm,** Doreen Cronin, Harry Bliss (illus.). Diary entries are punctuated with clever drawings that make them even funnier (making macaroni necklaces is accompanied by a group of worms, each tucked into a single piece of macaroni and looking proud) as this worm describes regular life underground and why he likes being a worm.

Keep reading. And keep reading FUN! It's a great habit. A ritual of a chapter a night, a chapter after dinner, or a long book to read aloud in the evening could carry you and your child through elementary school and beyond. As you read, you'll always have a point of connection, a shared experience that lies outside of your relationship as parent and child. Books will become, and remain, a beloved common ground.

First Chapterbooks to Share

- **Betsy-Tacy,** Maud Hart Lovelace, Lois Lenski (illus.). The first book in the series about two little girls in turn-of-the-century Wisconsin follows Betsy and Tacy through kindergarten, with familiar-feeling illustrations from Lenski. Holds the attention of boys and girls alike.

- **Ramona the Pest,** Beverly Cleary. Ramona's adjustment to kindergarten and her struggle to understand the confusing world will ring true for many preschoolers.

- **Charlie and the Chocolate Factory,** Roald Dahl. Charlie is just enough lighter and funnier than much of Dahl's work to be read to a fairly young child, and the entrancing word descriptions of the candy factory will fire up any imagination.

- **Little House in the Big Woods,** Laura Ingalls Wilder, Garth Williams (illus.). You probably remember this fairly gentle (but not without excitement) first book in the series, a look at a year in the life of young Laura and her family in pioneer Wisconsin. There's some bullet making and animal killing among the stories of Christmas stockings and sugaring, all of which may lead to some questions. You can answer or edit the text as you choose.

- **Flat Stanley,** Jeff Brown, Scott Nash (illus.). With only four simple chapters and plenty of illustrations, *Flat Stanley* makes a nice first chapter book, and its mixture of the routine and the extraordinary is timelessly appealing.

- **Mrs. Piggle Wiggle's Farm,** Betty MacDonald, Maurice Sendak (illus.). If you read these as a child you probably remember the magnificent silliness of Mrs. Piggle Wiggle's cures for childhood ailments like talking back and tattling, and that's what will capture your child's imagination. The adult conversations can be lengthy, didactic, and remarkably sexist, but they'll wash right over your child's head as she waits to get to the good part.

- **My Father's Dragon,** Ruth Stiles Gannett. A young boy rescues a young dragon from enslavement and rides him home. A nice starter adventure story with nothing scary about it and a good introduction to many of the familiar elements of fantasy.

- **Mr. Popper's Penguins,** Richard Atwater, Florence Atwater (illus.). Generations of kids have loved the tale of how Mr. Popper, a housepainter who dreams of exploring the South Pole, acquires a troop of trained penguins.

- **Just So Stories,** Rudyard Kipling. These are simply wonderful for reading aloud, oh best beloved. When your preschooler hits the "why" stage, there's nothing better than the story of how the overly curious baby elephant got his trunk.

- **Pippi Longstocking,** Astrid Lindgren, Louis S. Glanzman (illus.). Pippi is nine, red haired, strong as an ox, and lives all alone in her house with a horse and her monkey and nobody to tell her what to do. What child wouldn't want to hear more about that?

Appendix A:
Award Winners: The Caldecott and More

The Caldecott Medal

The Caldecott Medal was named in honor of nineteenth-century English illustrator Randolph Caldecott. It is awarded annually by the Association for Library Service to Children, a division of the American Library Association, to the artist of the most distinguished American picture book for children. The honored book often targets an older audience, as with the 2004 winner, Mordicai Gerstein for *The Man Who Walked Between the Towers*, but there are some wonderful winners and honor books (the runners-up) for babies and toddlers. Look for the familiar bronze medal or the silver honor shield. Here are some honorees we love:

- *Kitten's First Full Moon,* Kevin Henkes
- *Knuffle Bunny,* Mo Willems
- *Ella Sarah Gets Dressed,* Margaret Chodos-Irvine
- *Freight Train,* Donald Crews
- *In the Small, Small Pond,* Denise Fleming
- *Snowy Day,* Ezra Jack Keats
- *The Polar Express,* Chris Van Allsberg
- *When Sophie Gets Angry—Really, Really Angry...,* Molly Bang

The Charlotte Zolotow Award

The Charlotte Zolotow Award, recognizing outstanding writing in a picture book, is relatively new. Although the award is for the writing, all of the books honored offer wonderful illustrations as well, leading us to conclude that the committee is wisely looking at the whole book. (Similarly, you won't see the Caldecott go to a beautiful book with poor writing.) It's administered by the Cooperative Children's Book Center, a children's literature library of the School of Education, University of Wisconsin–Madison and appears as a gold seal with a rose on it. Molly Bang's *When Sophie Gets Angry—Really, Really Angry...* won this award as well as the Caldecott honor medal in 2000. Other winners (and honor books) we like for babies and toddlers:

- **Farfallina and Marcel,** Holly Keller
- **Five Creatures,** Emily Jenkins (author), Tomek Bogacki (illustrator)
- **The Night Worker,** Kate Banks (author), Georg Hallensleben (illustrator)
- **Snow,** Uri Shulevitz (also a Caldecott Honor Book)

The Kate Greenaway Medal

The Kate Greenaway Medal is awarded for distinguished illustration in a book for children published in the United Kingdom. Many of these books are also available in the United States. Unfortunately, for some reason (British reticence?) there's no outward display of the medal on winning books, although it's often mentioned in the back cover copy. Look for *I Will Not Ever Never Eat a Tomato*, by Lauren Child, and *The Baby Who Would Not Go to Bed*, by Helen Cooper.

The Coretta Scott King Award

The Coretta Scott King Award is presented annually by the Coretta Scott King Task Force of the American Library Association's Social Responsibilities Round Table. Recipients are authors and illustrators of African descent whose distinguished books promote an understanding and appreciation of the "American Dream." Winning books display a pyramid over a circle on a black and gold seal. These awards aren't limited to children's books, but a few stand-outs for our age group have been honored, like *Uptown*, by Bryan Collier, *Mufaro's Beautiful Daughters*, by John Steptoe, and *Wings* and *Black Cat*, by Christopher Myers.

Appendix B:
Resource Books and Websites

The following books and websites are excellent resources The list includes potentially useful links and supports for parents, care providers, and all those wishing more information about books for babies, toddlers, and twos. They include book publishers, libraries, and reviewers, teaching and parent-educational organizations.

Books and Magazines

- *The Read-Aloud Handbook: Fifth Edition,* Jim Trelease

- *Great Books for Babies and Toddlers: More Than 500 Recommended Books for Your Child's First Three Years,* Kathleen Odean

- *How to Get Your Child to Love Reading: For Ravenous and Reluctant Readers Alike,* Esmé Raji Codell

- *The Best Children's Books of the Year,* issued annually by the Bank Street College of Education, www.bankstreet.edu

- *The Horn Book Magazine,* www.hbook.com

- *100 Picture Books Everyone Should Know,* The New York Public Library, kids.nypl.org/reading

- *Ways of Telling: Conversations on the Art of the Picture Book,* Leonard S. Marcus, interviews with leading writers and illustrators

- *Babies Need Books: Sharing the Joy of Books with Children from Birth to Six,* Dorothy Butler

- *CCBC Choices,* an annual guide to the best children's books of the year, University of Wisconsin's Cooperative Children's Book Center, www.education.wisc.edu/ccbc

- *Talking with Artists,* Pat Cummings, three volumes of kid-friendly interviews with major children's book illustrators

- *Family Literacy from Theory to Practice,* Andrea DeBruin-Parecki, Barbara Krol-Sinclair, editors, academic and practical ideas for reading to children. Chapter 9 is Susan's contribution.

- *Inside Picture Books,* Ellen Handler Spitz, a thought-provoking look at the meanings books have for children

- *From Cover to Cover: Evaluating and Reviewing Children's Books,* Kathleen T. Horning, a how-to book

- *Every Child Ready to Read: Literacy Tips for Parents,* Lee Pesky Learning Center, focuses special interest on children with learning disabilities

Websites

- **American Library Association, Born to Read,** www.ala.org, a program for early reading

- **Zero-to-Three,** Washington DC, www.zerotothree.org, developmental information and resources; big supporter of babies

- **The Literacy Site,** www.theliteracysite.com and **First Book**, www.firstbook.org, information and help for getting books into the lives of families who need them

- **Multimedia Children's Literature Resource,** www.teachingbooks.com, resourceful for zero to teens

- **Beginning with Books, Center for Early Literacy,** www.beginningwithbooks.org, offers tips and titles

- **Reach Out and Read,** Boston, MA, www.reachoutandread.org, essentially a program to promote reading by pediatricians, offers reading tips and titles of note

- **Hennepin County Library,** Minnetonka, MN, www.hclib.org/BirthTo6, lots of wonderful selections for books and read-aloud tips, and further nursery rhyme and story websites

- **READ TO ME,** www.readtomeprogram.org, Susan's website for the READ TO ME Program that gets young families reading with their babies

Online Bookstores

- **The Book Vine for Children,** www.bookvine.com, a good source for recommendations and for packaged collections
- **Black Books Galore,** Toni Trent Parker, www.blackbooksgalore.com, features books for and by African Americans, starting with preschool titles
- **Amazon Books,** www.amazon.com
- **Barnes & Noble,** www.BN.com
- **Books of Wonder,** www.booksofwonder.net, excellent NYC-based independent bookstore
- **Powells Bookstore,** www.powells.com, excellent Oregon-based bookstore for new and used books
- **Abe Books,** www.abebooks.com, "Because you read"; great source for used and hard-to-find titles

Often, your favorite author or illustrator has a website. Rather than list them all, we suggest putting his or her name into a search engine and see what pops up. Write to let them know how valuable their work is in your life with your youngsters.

Index: BookLists

Chapter 10: Books to the Rescue: Potty Training, Food, Big Kid Beds, and More

Chapter 11: Reading Happily Ever After

About the Authors

Susan Straub is the founder and director of the READ TO ME Program, a series of workshops that encourage young families to read to their babies. Ms. Straub's work with READ TO ME has been celebrated on NY1 television network, in *O Magazine* and by Child Care, Inc. She lives in New York City with her husband and two cats.

KJ Dell'Antonia has written for many parenting publications, including *Parents*, *American Baby* and *Mothering*. She lives in New Hampshire with her husband, three small children, and two large dogs.

JUN 12 2008

OCT 21 2008

372.7